THE
SCHOOL
IMPROVEMENT
SPECIALIST
FIELD GUIDE

D1611341

THE
SCHOOL
IMPROVEMENT
SPECIALIST
FIELD GUIDE

DEB PAGE
JUDITH HALE

CORWIN
A SAGE Company

CORWIN
A SAGE Company

FOR INFORMATION:

Corwin
A SAGE Company
2455 Teller Road
Thousand Oaks, California 91320
(800) 233-9936
www.corwin.com

SAGE Publications Ltd.
1 Oliver's Yard
55 City Road
London, EC1Y 1SP
United Kingdom

SAGE Publications India Pvt. Ltd.
B 1/I 1 Mohan Cooperative Industrial Area
Mathura Road, New Delhi
India 110 044

SAGE Publications Asia-Pacific Pte. Ltd.
3 Church Street
#10-04 Samsung Hub
Singapore 049483

Acquisitions Editor: Arnis Burvikovs
Associate Editor: Desirée A. Bartlett
Editorial Assistant: Kimberly Greenberg
Production Editor: Amy Schroller
Copy Editor: Erin Livingston
Typesetter: Hurix Systems Pvt. Ltd.
Proofreader: Victoria Reed-Castro
Indexer: Maria Sosnowski
Cover Designer: Anupama Krishnan
Permissions Editor: Karen Ehrmann

Copyright © 2013 by Corwin

Printed in the United States of America.

Library of Congress Cataloging-in-Publication Data

Page, Deb.

The school improvement specialist field guide / Deb Page, Judith Hale.

pages cm

Includes bibliographical references and index.

ISBN 978-1-4522-4089-3 (pbk.)

1. School improvement programs—Handbooks, manuals, etc. 2. Educational leadership—Handbooks, manuals, etc. 3. School management and organization—Handbooks, manuals, etc. I. Hale, Judith A. II. Title.

LB2822.8.P23 2013

371.2'07—dc23

2012031313

This book is printed on acid-free paper.

Certified Chain of Custody
Promoting Sustainable Forestry
www.sfiprogram.org
SFI-01268

SFI label applies to text stock

12 13 14 15 16 10 9 8 7 6 5 4 3 2 1

Contents

Additional materials and resources related to
The School Improvement Specialist Field Guide
can be found on the companion website.
http://www.corwin.com/sisguide

List of Figures

List of Tools

Preface

AUDIENCE FOR THIS BOOK

As expectations and accountability for student learning and performance have risen over the last decade, a new educational role has evolved: the school improvement specialist (SIS). This book is intended to support people who facilitate improvement and transformation in schools or aspire to do so.

The SIS may be a person assigned from a government agency; a consultant hired to support a school, school district, or local education agency; an education administrator employed at the school or district level; or an instructional coach or teacher focused on systemic school improvement. Regardless of how the SIS came into this new role, his or her goal is to improve organizational processes and the performance of the adults who work in the organization to improve student achievement.

Often, an SIS is a former principal, school superintendent, or other education leader who may have been effective as an administrator, teacher leader, or counselor but who has little-to-no experience acting in a consultative or adult performance coaching role without direct authority over people or the organization. Typically, SIS will have to make many adjustments and acquire new skills to influence sustainable results, especially if they are expected to operate without direct authority over school staff.

Until the International Society for Performance Improvement (ISPI) codified the role of the SIS through the research of Page and Hale (International Society for Performance Improvement, 2012), the set of skills for this role was not standardized or documented. Anyone who could print a business card could claim to be a school improvement consultant or specialist. Using the outputs of the study conducted by Page and Hale in April 2010 the ISPI launched a new, fully evidence-based job certification for individuals who facilitate systemic school improvement—the Certified School Improvement Specialists (CSIS). The school improvement certification standards are also rooted in the ten human performance technology (HPT) standards, developed and refined by the ISPI over the last ten years. The HPT standards reflect the work of accomplished practitioners in both the private and public sectors of performance improvement.

Janie Fields is a CSIS who made the transition from the role of principal, leading a school, to the role of performance consultant, assigned to help other schools improve their performance.

> In my role as a principal, I led the turnaround of a low-performing school—a five-year process—[by] working with the faculty, staff and other administrators. When I was faced with the challenge of facilitating the improvement of schools where I was not the leader, I was not confident in my abilities. I had never been trained or prepared for the new role as a consultant. The organization I was working for, the Georgia Leadership Institute for School Improvement, brought in Dr. Judy Hale, who worked with us on understanding the role of a performance consultant and the methods for facilitation of improvement that is sustainable. At the time, I felt totally overwhelmed. As I did the work and followed what she taught, I began to see that there was a process for my work that would get the right results for those I was assigned to support. I am now an independent performance consultant, and I guide the schools and school districts who are my clients to improve their processes and performance so that student achievement improves and is sustainable. Every day, I use the tools that I now know are rooted in the field of Human Performance Technology and I apply the Certified School Improvement Specialist standards, the guideposts of my consulting work. I am proud to be a Certified School Improvement Specialist with evidence that I am proficient in the work my clients hire me to perform, and I am grateful that I now have access to a professional network of others who do the same work I do, around the country and around the world.

> When I participated in one of the focus groups that provided the information that resulted in the Certified School Improvement Specialist standards, I was pleased and proud to recognize that those of us who had been successful in facilitating school improvement were following similar processes, although we had adopted them independently. I was one of the only people in the group who had any formal training in facilitating improvement. That day, those of us in the group came to realize that we have a unique and valuable profession, with a

methodology that, when applied with fidelity, can facilitate others to produce sustainable improvement results. (J. Fields, CSIS, personal communication, August 12, 2011)

The School Improvement Specialist Field Guide describes the skills and knowledge required of effective school improvement professionals. It provides school improvement practitioners with examples, tools, and guidance they can use to develop their craft and reflect on their practice. This book will also help experienced practitioners prepare their applications for the CSIS certification.

Additional materials and resources related to
The School Improvement Specialist Field Guide
can be found on the companion website.
http://www.corwin.com/sisguide

Acknowledgments

We would like to acknowledge the special contributions to this book by Dr. Georgia G. Evans, CSIS; Ms. Janie Fields, CSIS; and Ms. Penelope Smith, CSIS. We also want to recognize the experts who shared their time and expertise to define their school improvement specialist profession and its standards and value and the experts who developed the standards and practice of human performance technology. Our special thanks goes to Dr. Edith E. Bell, CPT and Dr. Jeanne Schehl for contributing their time and expertise to the organization of the book. Finally, our thanks goes to Arnis Burvikovs for his confidence in supporting the publication of this book.

PUBLISHER'S ACKNOWLEDGMENTS

Corwin gratefully acknowledges the contributions of the following reviewers:

Betty Alford, Department Chair
Department Educational Leadership
Stephen F. Austin State University
Nacogdoches, TX

Patricia Conner, District Test Coordinator
Berryville Public Schools
Berryville, AR

Michael J. Dawkins, Regional Representative
School Administrators Association of New York State
Latham, NY

Susan Hudson, President
School Improvement Services
Nashville, TN

About the Authors

**Deb Page** is a strategy and performance consultant in systemic improvement of performance. She was awarded the evidence-based Certified Performance Technologist job certification in 2011 by the International Society for Performance Improvement (ISPI) based on her work in education improvement.

Deb and Dr. Judith Hale of **Hale Associates** (www.HaleAssociates.com) developed the fully evidence-based Certified School Improvement Specialist, awarded through a collaborative arrangement with the International Society for Performance Improvement (www.ISPI.org). Together they founded The Institute for Performance Improvement (www.TifPI.org), a social entrepreneurial organization that develops Communities of Practice of high performing practitioners to facilitate meaningful work and sustainable improvement in education and the workplace. The Institute trains individuals to effectively facilitate improvement using human performance technology (HPT).

Deb is a former K–12 educator who spent more than 20 years in corporate human capital management. She began her career as a high school teacher after graduating from the University of Georgia with a BS in Language Education. In 2001 she left her position as Sr. Vice President for Instruction and Business Development for Citibank, N.A. to form **Willing Learner, Inc.**

In 2002, she led the start of the Georgia Leadership Institute for School Improvement (www.GLISI.org) a public/private initiative to improve education leadership. Under her leadership the Institute developed a solid track record for helping school systems improve student achievement and organizational effectiveness.

Through her company, Willing Learner, Inc. she provides strategic planning support and performance consulting services. Contact Deb at deb.page@willinglearner.org or at 678–428–2363.

Judith Hale, PhD, CPT is one of ISPI's more prolific writers and well-known consultants in the field of performance improvement, certification, and sustaining major interventions. She is the author of *Performance-Based Certification: How to Design Valid, Defensible, Cost-Effective Program,* second edition (2012); *The Performance Consultant's Fieldbook: Tools and Techniques for Improving Organizations and People* second edition (2007); *Outsourcing Training and Development* (2006); *Performance-Based Management: What Every Manager Should Do to Get Results* (2003); and *Performance-Based Evaluation: Tools and Techniques for Measuring the Impact of Training* (2002). She has served as Director of Certification and President of ISPI. Judith was awarded a BA from Ohio State University in communications, a MA from Miami University in communications, and a PhD from Purdue University in instructional design. Her doctoral research was on how to control bias in competency studies.

Judy and Deb have launched a new venture—The Institute for Performance Improvement, L3C—dedicated to preparing professionals in the practice of human performance technology as it is applied to school improvement. They will apply project-based learning principles to help consultants (internal and external) to develop proficiency in performance improvement, performance consulting, evidence-based certification, and six 21st-century skills: Collaboration, Complex Communication, Critical Thinking and Problem Solving, Creativity, Comprehensive Digital Literacy, and Consultative Facilitation.

Introduction

THE PURPOSE OF THIS BOOK

This field guide is intended as a resource for those who facilitate school improvement by helping them (1) improve the effectiveness, quality, and efficiency of their work; (2) reduce the time they require to achieve competency, and (3) increase their confidence and pride in their professional practice.

Practitioners in general:	Practitioners seeking certification:
If you are interested in learning more about working with schools and school districts to improve the performance of students, teachers, and school leaders, this book will give you the tools and information you can use immediately.	If you currently work with schools and school districts and want to pursue certification as a way to have your work recognized, then this book will provide you with a deeper understanding of the criteria on which the Certified School Improvement Specialist (CSIS) credential is based. There is a "Readiness Assessment" that you can use to determine your readiness to apply for the CSIS certification.

APPLYING HUMAN PERFORMANCE TECHNOLOGY TO THE CERTIFICATION OF SCHOOL IMPROVEMENT SPECIALISTS

The International Society for Performance Improvement (ISPI) conducted a study in 2000–2001 to define the profession of performance improvement. It convened a cross-functional group whose membership represented the public and private sectors. The study resulted in ten standards for human performance technology (HPT) that formed the basis of the ISPI evidence-based certification, the Certified Performance Technologist (CPT). Figure I.1 summarizes the standards. To get to the full set of standards, go to http://www.ispi.org. The first four standards are principles. The last six describe the elements of the systematic process used by accomplished HPT practitioners (see Figure I.1).

1

Figure I.1   The HPT Standards

Principles:	Systematic Processes:
1. Focus on Results	5. Assess the Need or Opportunity
2. Take a Systems View	6. Analyze the Cause or Performance Requirements
3. Add Value	7. Design the Solution
4. Utilize Partnerships	8. Develop the Solution
	9. Implement the Solution
	10. Evaluate the Solution

HOW THE CERTIFICATION FOR SCHOOL IMPROVEMENT SPECIALISTS EVOLVED

Using the HPT standards as a starting document for common understanding of performance improvement, ISPI conducted a job-and-task analysis in 2009–2010 to identify what effective school improvement specialists do and what they must know. The process included inviting school improvement specialists with proven results to participate in structured group interviews or individual interviews. Participants had to have successfully improved school performance at the student level *and* the teacher, principal, or superintendent level and sustained the improvement for at least three years. The Nominal Group Technique (NGT) was used for the structured group interviews. The Critical-Incident technique was used for the individual interviews. The questions asked during the group interviews are listed in Figure I.2.

Figure I.2   Interview Questions

Assume the effective school improvement specialists (SIS) are consultants or assigned by the state or works in the county office:

- What do they do that makes them effective in their role?

- Is there a difference if the SIS is a principal?

- What do effective specialists in school improvement do that others who are less effective in that role fail to do or do not do well?

- What do specialists in school improvement know that makes them effective? What is their knowledge and expertise?

- What would you expect and accept as evidence of successful practice by an effective SIS?

This analysis was conducted based on the assumption that schools, school districts, states, nations, and provinces base their school improvement efforts on either an explicit reform or improvement model or tacit processes. The study defined the work of a school improvement specialist as the *facilitation* of those models or processes in a manner that leads to systemic and sustainable improvement.

Sustainable means the processes and improvement will continue *after* the school improvement specialist is no longer working with the school or district. *Systemic* reflects the process an effective school improvement specialist applies to study, improve, and align all the functions in the organization that ultimately impact student achievement. In HPT terms, the specialist focuses on the "work, workers, and workplace" of the school or school district, as shown in Figure I.3.

HOW THIS FIELD GUIDE IS ORGANIZED

There are ten chapters, and each chapter is dedicated to one of the standards that emerged from the results of the study. Each chapter contains examples of how the elements of the standard appear in practice. The chapters also contain tools and guidelines for doing the work. The names, characters, and incidents used in the stories throughout the book are fictitious, but their actions are derived from observations of real work in the field. Any resemblance to actual practitioners, living or dead, events, or locale is entirely coincidental. The end of the book contains resources and references for your use, as well as a readiness assessment for CSIS certification.

THE TEN STANDARDS

The following standards describe the work of proficient practitioners who facilitate adults working in schools and encourage school systems to adopt

Figure I.3   Focus of HPT

The Work—the processes, methods, activities, decisions, and efforts that create results and support teaching and learning

The Workers—students, teachers, school and district staff, administrators, coaches, partners, volunteers, and stakeholders who impact teaching and learning

The Workplace—the place where teaching and learning occurs and the context and culture that impact teaching and learning the behaviors and practices that improve the performance of students, teachers, and leaders.

Standard 1: Analyze and Apply Critical Judgment

1.1 Facilitate the collection, analysis, validation, and interpretation of quantitative and qualitative data regarding the multiple factors impacting student, teacher, leader, and school performance.

1.2 Demonstrate deep knowledge of the work of school improvement and transformation and the underlying research and best practices, particularly in improving curriculum, instruction, assessment, and facilitating solutions and breakthroughs.

1.3 Present evidence so that conclusions and solutions are supported and so that others have a clear model to follow.

Standard 2: Facilitate Deriving Meaning and Engagement

2.1 Help others create meaning from findings, research, and inquiry.

2.2 Help others comprehend the implications of their actions, recognize patterns, and accept new responsibilities.

2.3 Build supportive relationships among stakeholders by initiating and sustaining dialogue between individuals and groups.

2.4 Develop commitment so that people act in new ways, feel engaged, and believe change is possible.

Standard 3: Focus on Systemic Factors

3.1 Focus on the systemic and interdependent factors in the school context that impact students' learning, school improvement, and transformation efforts.

3.2 Demonstrate use and alignment of a portfolio of improvement options and approaches.

3.3 Ensure improvement and transformation efforts result in school teams and students demonstrating higher-order thinking skills, collaboration, effective use of technology, and other skills that create value.

Standard 4: Plan and Record

4.1 Recommend methods, resources, and high-impact practices and information about what works to address the factors impacting performance.

4.2 Facilitate development and recording of sound improvement and transformation plans with related action or project plans and progress measures.

4.3 Facilitate communicating the work ahead and the individual and team performance expectations so that people's efforts are aligned and focused on meaningful activities that are more likely to lead to the desired outcomes in support of student learning and school improvement and transformation.

4.4 Document the practices and progress so that best practices can be replicated with fidelity and taught and disseminated to others.

Standard 5: Organize and Manage Efforts and Resources

5.1 Organize work tasks by breaking them down into feasible steps.

5.2 Effectively distribute work, responsibility and accountability, authority, and leadership so that people are empowered and feel that their time is respected.

5.3 Coordinate efforts, schedules, and human and financial resources in ways that lead to important, agreed-on outcomes with effective stewardship of resources, including time.

Standard 6: Guide and Focus Collaborative Improvement

6.1 Influence the behaviors and decisions of stakeholders within a personal circle of influence.

6.2 Leverage the cooperation and support of others to influence a wider circle of stakeholders.

6.3 Facilitate the collaborative development of clear mission, vision, purpose, values, goals, and performance targets.

6.4 Provide relevant information and advice to support improvement, transformation, and sustainability.

6.5 Model the behaviors of continuous improvement and 21st-century transformation.

6.6 Facilitate or influence the tough decisions needed to achieve needed changes and breakthroughs.

Standard 7: Build Capacity

7.1 Use effective adult learning and performance interventions aligned to the desired outcomes and results.

7.2 Coach and provide feedback against clear criteria.

7.3 Ask questions that cause reflection so that others surface new possibilities and recognize self-imposed barriers.

7.4 Facilitate study, inquiry, and informed action that address complex challenges while working effectively with colleagues.

7.5 Facilitate sharing of learning that leads to improved practices, innovation, and positive change.

7.6 Facilitate adoption of defined and aligned practices in hiring, selection, assignment, development, and formative and summative performance evaluation that support improved performance of teachers, administrators, and staff.

Standard 8: Demonstrate Organizational Sensitivity

8.1 Establish professional credibility, gain respect, and build trust.

8.2 Follow accepted rules of etiquette, precedence, or conventions appropriate to the context.

8.3 Demonstrate a high level of professionalism through appropriate dress, speech, written communication, and behavior.

8.4 Interact in ways that make people feel their roles, positions, and views are valued.

8.5 Behave in ways that increase the likelihood that people stay engaged and honor their commitments.

Standard 9: Monitor Accountability and Adoption

9.1 Check purposely (keep an eye on) performance, conditions, and results by observing people's behavior and interim results.

9.2 Apply corrective action or refocus efforts, when needed, to reach the targeted performance and results.

9.3 Address underperformance or lack of progress toward goals and performance targets using data and evidence.

9.4 Recognize and communicate about effort, improvement, and achievements.

9.5 Ensure school improvement and transformation is aligned between schools and with the district office or management entity so that schools' efforts support systemwide improvement without undesirable impact on other schools.

Standard 10: Implement for Sustainability

10.1 Ensure continuity of interventions, fidelity of execution of plans, and sustainability of gains and improvements.

10.2 Establish and transfer ownership.

10.3 Facilitate evaluation of the effort.

10.4 Allow time for and gain support for long-term, sustainable improvement and transformation to meet 21st-century needs.

10.5 Solicit feedback to evaluate your own performance, and set goals for your own continued development.

Figure I.4 summarizes the CSIS Standards.

Figure I.4   Summary of CSIS Standards

1. Analyze and Apply Critical Judgment	6. Guide and Focus Collaborative Improvement
2. Facilitate Deriving Meaning and Engagement	7. Build Capacity
	8. Demonstrate Organizational Sensitivity
3. Focus on Systemic Factors	9. Monitor Accountability and Adoption
4. Plan and Record	
5. Organize and Manage Efforts and Resources	10. Implement for Sustainability

Although this field guide is organized by the ten standards, the work of school improvement is cyclical and is never a lockstep process. It requires continuous attention to data and feedback to inform and correct the course of action.

ISPI adopted the same Code of Ethics for the CSIS designation as used in the CPT credential (Figure I.5). Collectively, it is intended to promote ethical practice in the work of performance improvement.

Figure I.5   Code of Ethics

The Code of Ethics reads:

1. **Add Value Principle**

   Strive to conduct yourself and manage your projects and their results in ways that add value for your clients, their customers, and the global environment.

2. **Validated Practice Principle**

   Make use of and promote validated practices in performance technology strategies in keeping with the Standards of Performance Technology.

3. **Collaboration Principle**

   Work collaboratively with clients and users, functioning as a trustworthy strategic partner.

4. **Continuous Improvement Principle**

   Continually improve your proficiency in the field of performance technology.

5. **Integrity Principle**

   Be honest and truthful in your representations to clients, colleagues, and others with whom you may come in contact with while practicing performance technology.

6. **Uphold Confidentiality Principle**

   Maintain client confidentiality, not allowing for any conflict of interest that would benefit you or others.

APPLICATION FOR CERTIFICATION

A school improvement practitioner can earn the evidence-based CSIS job certification by submitting an online application at http://www.ispi.org. The application must document a systemic improvement project the applicant facilitated, supported by a client or employer attestation and at least three years of triangulated performance data. The data must reflect the wide range of factors in the work, workers, and workplace that were addressed through the improvement initiative. Modeled after the CPT double-blind review process, the CSIS review process masks both the identity of the applicant and the reviewers. The reviewers are experts who hold either a CPT designation or a CSIS designation (or both).

CSIS PERFORMANCE FOUNDATIONS

A design team of CSIS collaborated to develop a mission, vision, set of values, and criteria for effective performance for their profession.

Mission

We facilitate the adults in schools to improve processes and performance so that all students can achieve at high levels.

Vision

School improvement specialists are professionals with proven proficiency in the body of work represented in the Certified School Improvement Specialist standards.

Values

We believe that
- people can grow and change.
- problems are more process-related than people-related.
- most people want to do a good job.
- the key to improvement is rooted in relationships.
- influence, not power, creates meaningful change.
- the school improvement process must be embedded in the culture of the school and become "how we do things around here" to produce sustainable improvement.

Performance Criteria

Sustainable improvement after we leave is the evidence of our success.

During the development of the CSIS standards, those interviewed overwhelmingly agreed that they had never received structured training or support in the craft of their work. Therefore, *The School Improvement Specialist Field Guide* is designed to support and guide school improvement practitioners in effectively facilitating school improvement while meeting the ten standards established by ISPI. To find out about other educational and professional development opportunities, go to The Institute for Performance Improvement's website: http://www.tifpi.org.

Analyze and Apply Critical Judgment

1

Bailey Pittman knew that changing her role from a high school principal to a performance consultant assigned to facilitate the improvement of another high school with a 56 percent graduation rate would be challenging. Over the last five years, she had led her school team to turn around the performance of her school (a persistently low-achieving school) to become a high-performing school recognized with many performance awards. However, Bailey knew that each school is unique and was eager to discover what was holding this school back. She knew that one of her colleagues, Frank Perez, whom she had attended graduate school with, had made the switch from leading a school to performance consulting nearly five years ago. The week before starting in her new role, Bailey decided to call Frank and ask his advice about the job transition.

Frank was delighted to hear from Bailey and eager to share what he had learned. "I know you are going to do a great job in your new role," Frank said. "I would be happy to tell you what I have learned and experienced. Many of us who make this transition were high performers in leading schools; however, being a consultant or school improvement specialist is somewhat different than being a school leader. In an underperforming school, it is likely that those who work in the school have seen many people come and go who were attempting to help. Also, if you do not have direct authority over the people working in the school, you have to influence the improvements, not order them to be implemented. In order to support the types of changes needed to improve the performance of a school like the one you are assigned to help, it is important to get them to focus on the facts and guide them in identifying the gap between where they are and where they could be, all while building trust and good relationships. What I learned was that although all schools have similarities, all also have unique contexts that impact their performance and the achievement of their students."

"Don't make the mistake I made in the beginning of my transition." Frank cautioned. "I thought that because I had turned around the school I led, I knew

how to fix the first school I was assigned to help. I soon learned to study all the data and information and develop some hypotheses based on my experience and existing research before engaging the people in the school. I had to take time to listen, observe, and learn with them to truly get a clear picture of the state of the school. I have learned quite a bit over the past five years. Upon reflection, I have realized that what made me effective in leading improvement of my own school was that I was a collaborative leader and facilitated change, rather than ordering compliance. Both as a leader and a consultant assigned to a school, I had to take the time to identify the unique challenges and strengths within the school before recommending changes."

"Recently, I earned the Certified School Improvement Specialist job certification. I did that by documenting my work in facilitating school improvement and the results. During the application process, I did a great deal of reflection on the craft of facilitation of school improvement, and I developed a network of people who were pursuing their certification who I can now reach out to for advice when I have a challenge or want to share something I am working on and get ideas from others. If you would like, I will be happy to connect you with that network. You are going to be very successful, and I know you will really enjoy the work ahead. Feel free to call me anytime."

Story to be continued . . .

In your role as a school improvement specialist, the focus is always on others—those you are guiding and the students they serve. However, as you make your journey through this book, you are invited to enjoy a rare professional experience—focusing on *you*. Whether you are a leader in a school or an external expert charged with improving and transforming schools to support student success, you spend your time focused on helping, teaching, guiding, and supporting others. This book is about you, your craft of facilitating improvement, and your success. School improvement is a collaborative effort, where the focus is on the students, faculty, staff, administrators, and other stakeholders but never on you. This book is intended to allow you to reflect, learn, and focus on becoming more effective so that you can succeed in helping those you guide and support to be more successful.

This book will also help you compare your day-to-day efforts, performance, and results to the Certified School Improvement Specialist (CSIS) standards; however, it is intended to support you in increasing your skills and knowledge and your appreciation of the unique and valuable role you play in schools independent of whether you choose to pursue certification. Enjoy this opportunity to focus and reflect on *you!*

STANDARD 1: ANALYZE AND APPLY CRITICAL JUDGMENT

The first CSIS standard, *Analyze and Apply Critical Judgment,* reflects the work you must do in preparation to guide and engage others in systemic improvement efforts. The work begins with the collection and study of the data and artifacts that provide insight into the systemic factors impacting school and student performance. This analysis and critical review prepares you to identify and address the barriers in the work and workplace that may impede the adoption of new behaviors and improved practices and establish a culture that is enduring and supports success for all. Just as Bailey Pittman was about to experience a role transition, you have made this change or will experience it. How you manage your entrance into the organization or group you will facilitate and the analysis and thinking you apply initially will play a large part in your ability to support the needed changes in a school.

If you have been appointed to serve as a school improvement specialist or have inherited the role (possibly along with other responsibilities), it is important to realize that you are a performance consultant, someone who is

- an expert in performance analysis and measurement, who facilitates sustainable improvement, typically without authority over the individuals he or she is guiding.
- able to facilitate those who work in the organization to take responsibility for improving performance.
- unbiased and not predisposed toward a particular solution, using data to guide recommendations and decisions.
- skilled in guiding conversations that keep those who work in the organization engaged and focused on improvement, meaningful outcomes, and results.

Your job is a blend of the role of expert and facilitator. You are performing your job because someone assumes you are an expert, with knowledge from past practice in improving school performance, someone who has the skills needed to advise and guide others to improve and the facilitation skills to guide group processes, manage group dynamics, and support the change process. You are expected to bring the interpersonal skills and the abilities needed to bring people to consensus, to manage conflict, and to simultaneously provide pressure and support with a level of neutrality that reflects fairness and a belief that improvement is both possible and required.

> You are expected to bring the interpersonal skills and the abilities needed to bring people to consensus, to manage conflict, and to simultaneously provide pressure and support with a level of neutrality that reflects fairness and a belief that improvement is both possible and required.

Facilitating the Collection and Interpretation of Data

The focus of the first element of Standard 1 is on how you should immerse yourself in performance data to understand the unique issues and strengths within the school before engaging others in the improvement process.

1.1 Facilitate the collection, analysis, validation, and interpretation of quantitative and qualitative data regarding the multiple factors impacting student, teacher, leader, and school performance.

Understanding the data yourself will ensure that you are prepared to help others appropriately use the data they already have, question the relevance and utility of the data to support improvement, validate the data to confirm they accurately reflect what is intended, and interpret the meaning or implications of the data. You must collect and study both qualitative and quantitative data. *Qualitative* data are perceptions and attributes that may be ordered by source or impact. *Quantitative* data are numbers and measurements. Qualitative data are sometimes referred to as *soft data* and quantitative data as *hard data*; however, what makes data soft is that the perceptions are not independently verifiable (Guerra-Lopez, 2008). Similarly, what makes data hard is not that it is made up of numbers and measures but that it is verifiable through external sources (Kaufman, Guerra, & Platt, 2006).

This analysis and critical review allows you to

- develop an understanding of the systemic, "as-is" state of the performance of the school, administrators, teachers, staff, and students.
- identify the barriers in the work, workers, and workplace that are limiting improvement as well as the strengths to be leveraged.
- determine the gap between current behaviors, capacity, practices, and results and those that are expected, required, and valued.
- scan the culture and identify the underlying assumptions and beliefs that are limiting improvement as well as those that can be leveraged to support improvement and transformative change.

- prepare to engage administrators and others who will be coached to lead the change process by facilitating collection and analysis and then clearly identifying the needs and opportunities so that understanding and ownership can be established over time.
- assess your own biases and begin the process of establishing credibility.

To be an effective school improvement specialist, you must focus on outcomes and measurable results and display working knowledge of data collection, analysis, and measurement in schools, including the various types of data that

- are readily available in schools and school districts.
- will require additional effort, tools, and processes to collect.
- will support the study of causal relationships and leading or predictive indicators of performance.
- give insight into the processes and performance factors that impact student achievement.

The collection and analysis of data usually begins with reviewing the data that are publicly available from state or national testing organizations and annual reports and then analyzing that data against any existing school improvement plans. You want to become familiar with the data that those who work in the school or school district can or should be able to see. Your focus will also be on determining if a school's plans correctly reflect its performance improvement needs.

This review of multiple types of qualitative and quantitative data includes existing data in a few categories, such as student achievement, demographics, perceptions and engagement, and process data. Figure 1.1, though not exhaustive, suggests types of data in each category.

Figure 1.1   Examples of Data

Student Achievement Data:

- Overall summative school achievement data such as state test data; graduation rates; student grade-to-grade, school-to-school, and ability level promotion rates; SAT test scores; college progression; career readiness; or value-added measures of learning, which indicate if a student is achieving a full year of learning for a full year of instruction

(Continued)

Figure 1.1   (Continued)

- Disaggregated summative student achievement, organized by student groups
- Multiple assessments—interim assessments, such as weekly tests against the standards of the curriculum taught; formative assessments (also known as *assessments for learning*), such as writing assignments that indicate which standards a student has mastered to date to determine if the instructional interventions are working; and summative assessments, which reflect the levels of learning achieved after a course of instruction is completed
- Similar schools' performance compared to this school's performance
- Review of student work against standards

Demographic Data:

- School demographic data
- Community demographic data

Perception and Engagement Data:

- Student attendance
- Student engagement
- Parent/family engagement
- Teacher attendance
- Teacher engagement
- Other external stakeholder engagement
- Partner engagement

Process Data:

- Professional learning
- Teacher, staff, and administrator performance data
- Student behavior data, such as student discipline referrals
- Talent, such as the degrees held by teachers relative to their teaching assignments
- Nutrition, such as students' access to protein-rich foods early in the day
- Financial management, such as forecasting and tracking budgets and expenses
- Maintenance, such as preventative care and life cycle analysis of equipment
- Transportation, such as optimizing bus stops to reduce fuel costs and increase safety

- Scheduling, such as providing common planning time for teams of teachers across the curriculum
- Instructional technology, such as the use of electronic portable devices to collect student responses in classrooms
- Management technology, such as staff and parent information portals or security and attendance systems
- Special education, such as the quality of inclusion co-teaching
- Student support services, such as alignment of after-school programs with community resources
- Observations in standards-based classrooms
- Alignment of curriculum, classroom instruction, and assessments.
- Quality of student assignments compared to 21st-century skills and curriculum standards
- The degree of focus on reading and writing instruction across the curriculum
- Horizontal and vertical alignment of processes and practices—school-to-school, grade-to-grade, class-to-class
- Dual secondary and university enrollments, advanced placement, International Baccalaureate, career and technical participation, acceleration programs, credit recovery, internships, work-based learning

Once you have identified the sources and types of data to be analyzed, the *Guidelines for Analyzing Data* (Tool 1.1) provide questions you can use to analyze the data initially available to you. A great deal of data exists for every school. Once you have collected it, it may help to group the data by purpose or intent so you can identify themes and corroborating examples.

From the initial analysis, you will have to determine whether additional data will be needed to facilitate teachers, administrators, and principals in recognizing the need to improve performance and to take responsibility for that improvement. By using the early phase of data collection and analysis to understand needs and gaps, you demonstrate to school personnel that you are focusing on results and outcomes and you set the tone for engaging them in getting the facts, measuring their own results, and strategically planning for improved performance. By demonstrating that you are looking for data and performance factors that are wider and deeper than just state or national test scores, you can help facilitate understanding that school improvement is complex work that requires an aligned suite of systemic solutions to produce real and sustainable improvement. Figure 1.2 illustrates the process of moving from working with available data to collecting additional data required to identify the gaps in the processes that support improvement and that guide prioritization.

Tool 1.1   Guidelines for Analyzing the Data

Guidelines: Use the following set of questions to help you reflect on the data you have available and how to best use that data as you move forward.

1. What does each particular data set measure?

2. Do the data reflect a particular point in time or an accumulation of points over time?

3. How do the data within a set support or refute each other?

4. What other data exist that might add clarity?

5. Where might you get data to verify your initial conclusions?

Next, to better understand the data, ask:

6. Have the data changed? Is there a trend?

7. What are the implications if future data demonstrate a continuation of the trend?

8. What other data exist that may give insight to what is contributing to the results you are seeing?

Figure 1.2   Collecting and Analyzing Data

Collection and Analysis of Available Achievement, Demographic, Perception, and Process Data

Areas of Need Identified

Collection and Analysis of Data Not Captured or Tracked By Available Systems or More Specific Data Required to Determine and Prioritize Needs

The focus on inquiry and data centers the attention on the discovery of facts rather than assumptions. Whether or not you have been directly responsible for past performance of the school, you might have assumptions about what causes poor performance based on your experience in other schools or organizations. Warning! The tools and techniques in this field guide are meant to help you facilitate change and improvement and apply and validate the expertise you can effectively bring to bear, but it is critical that you work from facts and data rather than intuition or assumptions.

> Warning! The tools and techniques in this field guide are meant to help you facilitate change and improvement and apply and validate the expertise you can effectively bring to bear, but it is critical that you work from facts and data rather than intuition or assumptions.

Combining analysis with critical judgment before engaging those you will guide will help you avoid the trap of jumping to solutions before entirely understanding the gap between where the school is and where it needs to be and why that gap exists. Reviewing the data that are publically available about a school only provides a partial view into the factors impacting performance and results in a school or school district. You will want to collect additional data before forming your own hypotheses.

Your inquiry must reflect a lack of bias and a willingness to deeply and truly understand what is going on in the school and what is impacting the *work* (teaching and learning), the *workers* (students, faculty, support staff, administrators, instructional coaches, paraprofessionals, and other stakeholders), and the *workplace* (the places where the work of teaching and learning is situated, including within the community and the student's family). For example, independent initial analysis of data followed by effective questioning techniques can produce additional information as well as build trust and acceptance by those you are questioning and will later engage in the improvement process. You must also pay close attention to the interpersonal and political factors at play, choosing carefully who you interview and in what order, so that the leaders of the school, teachers, and support staff perceive that you are honoring their roles, authority, and points of view.

No matter what your past experiences in school improvement may have been or your impressions of the school or what you have read and studied about schools, the school you are supporting has a unique context, with multiple and unique performance factors. Your first and primary task is to set aside assumptions, hunches, and opinions and study the school and its performance in an unbiased fashion. You must be willing and able to pursue a systematic inquiry process to determine what is contributing to school performance and what is impeding it. Your job is not to *assume* what is happening, why it is happening, and how to fix it but to *find out* what, why, and how it is happening before attempting to propose solutions or take action. Using data and seeking facts shows that you are setting assumptions aside and prepares those you will guide to later accept your expert opinions because you have established yourself as a neutral performance investigator.

By focusing on multiple types of data, you will demonstrate that you understand that student performance is impacted by a host of internal and external factors. The state of an underperforming school is what cognitive experts term an *ill-structured problem*. Ill-defined or ill-structured problems are "those that we encounter in everyday life, in which one or several aspects of the situation are not well specified, the goals are unclear, and there is insufficient information to solve them" (Ge & Land, 2004, p. 5).

Being an effective school improvement specialist requires showing that you bring with you a disciplined approach and body of practice to study and address the ill-structured problem of an underperforming school. You must demonstrate your intention and expertise to assess performance; identify performance factors; select, recommend, and evaluate the right interventions; and facilitate the collection of process and performance data to evaluate the effectiveness of interventions. Finally, you must demonstrate that you can facilitate others to implement interventions with fidelity and adopt new behaviors. The starting point for establishing yourself as a credible expert begins with the work of collecting data and facts and seeking first to understand those data and facts in a manner that leads others to become willing to understand these data, accept that changes are needed, and respond favorably to you in your performance consulting role.

Dr. Georgia Evans is a highly effective CSIS who has supported the turnaround and systemic, ongoing improvement of many schools in varied contexts. She stresses the importance of questioning and collecting data and information using methods that build engagement, help those who lead and work in the school avoid embarrassment, eliminate blaming, and increase the odds that she will be able to facilitate improvement.

> I thoroughly review all the publically available data on schools I am assigned to support in advance of my first visit. I want to have as much understanding of the current state of performance as possible, but I never walk in with a preformed opinion of the school's needs or a plan. My initial review of data before entering the school or school district simply helps me know all I can before I learn the rest of what I need to know to facilitate those doing the work of schooling to make improvements. The analysis process is like putting a puzzle together. I know I only have some of the pieces of the puzzle when I arrive at the school for the first time. I have seen many improvement consultants and school leaders who limit their effectiveness in facilitating sustainable improvement, because they arrive with a plan, with solutions they think are needed, and

with strong opinions. Doing this role well requires paying close attention to *how* I perform the initial inquiry and study.

My questioning process helps me find missing pieces of the performance puzzle, which can only be obtained by methodical questioning in an order that respects the leadership, teachers, and all who impact student success. (G. Evans, personal communication, August 10, 2011)

After her initial independent review of the school's data, Evans uses an interview protocol that follows a structured process as shown in the *Initial Inquiry Worksheet* (Tool 1.2). She typically begins by talking with supervisors of the school, then moves on to the lead principal or headmaster, and gradually connects with the entire leadership team, including assistant principals, instructional coaches, groups of teachers, counselors, and other support staff. She records their answers and uses her initial independent inquiry to compare the perceptions of those she interviews to what she has identified in her preliminary work as strengths, needs, and evidence.

I ask everyone the same questions—[including] students who are old enough to provide answers—and then compile and analyze their answers. After each interview, I compare their answers to their school improvement initiatives. I want to know if the needs shared with me are the same as those in their school improvement plans and if they are aligned. My goal is to not only understand what they see as strengths and improvement needs, but to let them see that I am both truly interested in their perspectives and committed to validating and corroborating their points of view. Later, I will lead them to dig deeper into the data and evidence, because I will need to help each person and group understand the rationale behind [the] needed changes. (G. Evans, personal communication, August 10, 2011)

Once you have completed your interviews, you can compile areas of strength and improvement using a *Plus-Delta Chart*, as shown in Tool 1.3.

Evans next conducts classroom observations and uses checklists to turn her observations into quantitative data, such as the number of classrooms she visited that were using differentiated instruction or the number of teachers who were using instructional practices aligned to the performance or curriculum standards for their teaching content. Evans emphasizes the primacy of improvement specialists' knowledge of the core business of schools, teaching, and learning as a part of their body of expertise:

Tool 1.2   Initial Inquiry Worksheet

Guidelines: This worksheet is meant for you to modify to meet your own needs. It can help you discover the group's beliefs about the school and what they are using as evidence to support their beliefs.

Site: _____ Interviewee/Group:_____

Title/role: _____Contact: _____

What do you believe are the strengths of this school (or school district)?	Why do you think these strengths exist?	What data or evidence can you point to that proves that?
What do you think are the areas in need of improvement that currently exist?	Why do you think these areas in need of improvement exist?	What data or evidence can you point to that proves that?

Tool 1.3   Plus-Delta Chart

Guidelines: This is a chart you will want to build on as you continue your work with the school. It is not intended to be a onetime activity, but one that encourages everyone to record their new insights as they continue down the journey of school improvement.

+ 's = Areas of Strength	Δ's = Areas of Improvement

A capable school improvement specialist must have expert knowledge of effective curriculum, instruction, and assessment standards to be able to observe classroom performance and translate what is seen and heard into data that can support the improvement process. (G. Evans, personal communication, August 10, 2011)

Demonstrating Deep Knowledge

Evans' belief in the necessity of expert thinking is supported by the second element of Standard 1:

> 1.2 Demonstrate deep knowledge of the work of school improvement and transformation and the underlying research and best practices, particularly in improving curriculum, instruction, assessment, and facilitating solutions and breakthroughs.

This element focuses on your expertise in the core work of schools—providing the right curriculum, instruction, and assessment—as well as your expertise in taking a disciplined approach to assessing and guiding the effectiveness of the work performed. Your expertise must include the ability to focus upon factors in the school and its environment that are unrelated to the core work but that impact teaching and learning. Schools are affected by their place within a system of schools and their community as well as what is taking place in the state, the region, the nation, and the world. Your expertise in the delivery of curriculum, instruction, assessment, and student support amid a powerful confluence of changing social, political, economic, demographic, and technological factors is essential.

The nature of the work of school improvement, driven by the moral imperative to help all students succeed, as well as local, state, and national mandates place you in the best of all and the worst of all situations: You are there to help, guide, coach, and support others as they accept responsibility, change, and improve; and you are there to point out and bring the organization to address what is missing or not working and who is not performing to required and expected levels. Reform mandates may have landed you in the unenviable position of being "from the district office/state/government/outside and here to help." Persistently underperforming schools have seen folks arrive and depart before and have managed to intentionally or unintentionally resist change.

In addition to your role as facilitator, aiding and supporting those within the school to understand the gaps and needs and to assume ownership and accountability for results, your role requires proficiency in several expert areas:

1. Researcher: Identify, develop, or test data and information and translate its implications for improved performance.

2. Guide in Research-Based Practices: Illustrate and assist in understanding and adopting practices with fidelity that have produced improvement in schools with similar contexts and performance factors.

3. Compliance Analyst: Identify and document gaps in performance which result in the organization being out of compliance with local, state, provincial, or national laws, rules, and regulations.

4. Needs Analyst: Identify ideal and existing performance, conditions, and causes.

5. Trainer: Teach those who work in the school to perform their work to the required performance standards and encourage them to develop capability, which will allow them to be successful when you are no longer working with them.

6. Subject Matter Expert: Draw on professional knowledge, skills, resources, and expertise.

7. Coach: Support on-the-job practices, provide clear performance criteria and feedback on performance, devote time to others' performance needs, focus attention and resources on their behalf, support problem solving and other skills necessary for others to achieve optimal performance.

Becoming an effective school improvement specialist requires fluency in the multiple roles that establish your expertise and opens others' minds to valuing your points of view and practices. Most important, to establish expert value in the minds of others, they must perceive you as contributing value that they cannot produce on their own. If they believe they already know what you know, can do what you do, have access to the same resources as you, and have the time and level of attention to needs and solutions that you bring, they cannot and will not value your contributions as an expert, facilitator, or consultant. Being recognized as a valued, credible expert means establishing a gap in their perception between what they bring to the table and what you can bring, so they feel they need your help and are willing to go with you on the journey of improvement. In later chapters, we will explore other methods for building credibility, in addition to establishing value as a school improvement expert and effective performance consultant.

Dr. Evans points to the need for teachers and administrators to see that as an observer and facilitator of performance, you have the same or a deeper knowledge of the system of teaching and learning and are not guided by a narrow research base.

I have learned that it is essential to know the research concerning teaching and learning, but I know I must be careful how I reference research. During teachers' preparation, they may have encountered professors who focus deeply on a single area of research, and the teachers may perceive those professors as biased by their narrow academic focus, causing teachers to question the value of academic research in the complex real world of schools. I usually don't talk about research-based best practices until after my initial data collection from classroom observations so that practice and academic research are informing both our discovery and interpretation.

I am careful to always leave at least a brief thank you note on the door of every teacher I observe and note at least one good research-based practice I saw. I want them to know that I know what good instruction looks like and that I am seeking to learn and understand, not to tell them what they are doing wrong or should do. I work to identify the capacity and capability of every adult in the school, and later, I use this information as I facilitate groups working together, drawing on each individual's strengths. This is part of the "gathering of the puzzle pieces," and I know [at this point] it is too soon to make recommendations.

I let my knowledge of research and my experience inform my inquiry at the initial stages. Next, I use it to inform my critical judgment about what to present to the group to bring the school team along with me on the improvement journey. (G. Evans, personal communication, August 10, 2011)

Presenting Evidence That Supports Conclusions

The last element of Standard 1 focuses on the way that you communicate what you and others have discovered so that the expertise you bring to bear is valued, your intentions are viewed as honorable and trustworthy, and you are established as an effective guide toward what is needed, possible, and required.

> 1.3 Present evidence so that conclusions and solutions are supported and so that others have a clear model to follow.

You have choices about how you present the data and your findings so others will accept your intentions and ask for your help. Whatever approach you choose, you want others to recognize the implications, ask better questions than they would have without data to inform their inquiry, and be willing to discuss potential actions that will improve student and school performance. For example, when presenting the data, consider commenting aloud what questions the data raised for you, how the data made you wonder about what the contributing factors were, and what data might corroborate your initial suspicions.

Evans follows a protocol for presenting what she has found that helps her to demonstrate her willingness to listen and understand while guiding the focus toward improvement needs that her audience will later agree to own. She stresses making sure the principal or headmaster has the first opportunity to review the findings and has a choice to review it first or to engage others:

> I begin with the principal or headmaster by saying, "I have collected some data and have some observations. I would like to share them with you and anyone else you would like in the first conversation. I will eventually need to share this with all the school team and your supervisor, but I want to meet with everyone on a schedule that you choose between now and our deadline for the initial inquiry phase. If you are ready to begin that process, how would you like to proceed?" (G. Evans, personal communication, August 10, 2011)

By giving school leaders a choice regarding who first reviews the initial findings, you help the leader trust your intentions and you position the leader as a part of the team working on the improvement, which you are assigned to facilitate. If you are required to share the findings first with his or her supervisor, make sure the principal or headmaster knows this is not within your control and that you are committed to his or her success. Stress that school improvement is owned by a school team and its supervisors and support staff, not just the school's leader or leadership team.

The presentation of evidence and data need not be complex; however, sometimes data are best presented formally, as in a report or through graphics. Other times, data are best presented informally or offered in a spontaneous fashion, for example, by putting them on a white board or flipchart paper. In both cases, data have more meaning if they are combined with corroborating data. Where possible, put data in sequence to show a trend. Support the data with other information that illustrates changes or other dynamics.

Your goals at the beginning of a school improvement initiative are to create understanding for both yourself and the school team and supervisors and to create engagement that will support needed changes. Later, you will dig deeper to find root causes and, eventually, solutions. How you present the data and engage the client initially is critical to gaining trust, demonstrating your good intentions, and helping others believe you can help them "get there" and be successful.

Your data presentation must reinforce the points you need to make and convince the client of the benefit of working toward improvement.

Most important, you must help others see that change will happen and that they will be part of the success story.

Because your goal is engagement, presenting initial data is only a prelude to the actual collection of data and information that can point to possible solutions. Those who work in the school must be engaged in the study of data and must learn how to access and use data to achieve and sustain improvement. Handing teachers and administrators their data and analyzing it for them is not as likely to engage them in improvement efforts as giving them enough data to challenge their assumptions and convince them to dig deeper.

Teachers and school administrators, like all adult workers, must understand the rationale behind what they are expected to do and achieve. As you are presenting your findings, build a case for why things must change and improve by helping your audiences see the gap between what is and what can be and between what they think the current levels of performance are and what they actually are.

Evans describes a simple tool, the *Assumptions Worksheet* in Tool 1.4, which she uses during and after her presentation of findings to achieve agreement in the need to change.

> I post a large sheet of paper that has a grid showing the highest scores, state average scores, and lowest scores. Next, I set out self-stick notes or colored stickers and ask them to individually mark on the paper their answers to the question, "Where do you think our school *could be* in comparison to the state average—below, at, or above?" If I think it will help, I will sometimes show how the school or district demographics compare with the state's demographics; for example, I might say, "Our school population is 23 percent Hispanic compared to 26 percent of the state population. The meet and exceed percents for our Hispanic/Latino students in 4th grade math is 57 percent compared to 78 percent of Hispanic students at the state level."
>
> Once we have completed the marked sheet, we use it to discuss their expectations as compared with what the data say about the school's actual position. For example, if the school is below the state in math performance and they believe it should be above the state, then it is easier for them to agree something needs to change.
>
> The rationale I use is that educators want their students to do well relative to their peers in other places. So far, I have never seen any group of educators go through this exercise and agree they do not want their students to exceed the average. I know that our goal is to help every student succeed at high levels, so the exercise is not about setting an exact performance target but about agreeing that improvement is needed and that we want our students to be the best.

This challenges apathy, excuses, and the status quo. Even in areas where students exceed the state average, I ask, "Do you want your students to do better than they are doing and if so, how well?" Later we can investigate why students are performing as they are, using data and evidence. My goal is to get everyone in agreement that change and improvement are needed and to influence them to let me facilitate them through the change and improvement process. I also use this process to compare student graduation, college enrollment rates, and performance on national tests such as the SAT and ACT. (G. Evans, personal communication, August 10, 2011)

Tool 1.4   Assumptions Worksheet

Guidelines: This tool is designed to help you elicit the group's assumptions about the school in terms of how it compares to other schools in the district, state, or nation. You may edit this worksheet to reflect the entities against which you are comparing your school.

Consider where you think your school/district should be in comparison to the state. Place a mark on the chart indicating where you would place your school/district.

Highest Scores in State

State Average on _____ (whatever test or performance data you are analyzing)

Lowest Scores in State

Reflection questions:

1. Based on the group's response to the chart, what observations can we make?

2. How can this information help guide our discussion of test data?

3. How do you think the rest of the school would respond to this same exercise?

Another useful tool, the *Demographic Comparison Chart* (as shown in Tool 1.5), helps you prepare to guide the group to come to their own conclusions about the need for change and improvement. Adapt this chart to reflect the student subgroups within the school or schools you are supporting.

Tool 1.5   Demographic Comparison Chart

Guidelines: Use or edit this tool to reflect the demographic factors relevant to your school to help the group find out how their school's performance compares to other schools.

Review the demographic data below.

1. What is the performance of each subgroup?

2. Where do you think we should be?

3. How can understanding our demographics guide us in our efforts to improve our overall performance?

Demographics	Our School	State Averages
White		
African American		
Hispanic/Latino		
Native American		
Asian/Pacific Islander		
Multiracial/Other		
Students with Disabilities		
English Language Learners		
Gifted		
Free- and Reduced-Lunch Qualified		

Similarly, the *Performance Comparison Chart*, shown in Tool 1.6, can be used to illustrate the school's performance in academic areas as compared to the state or other standards. Use the chart to both communicate what the data say and what others believe is possible. Your goal is to get commitment to change, not to assign blame.

While Standard 1 represents the work that is performed at the initial stages of inquiry in a school improvement initiative, the work is iterative and recursive in nature. The performance consultant leading school improvement uses the three elements of Standard 1 throughout the improvement cycle to

Tool 1.6   Performance Comparison Chart

Guidelines: Use or edit this tool to compare a specific school's performance by subject area to the state's averages.

Subject and Grade Level	Our School	State Averages
English and Language Arts		
Math		
Science		
Social Studies		

- facilitate the collection and study of data so that the right conclusions can be reached to inform judgments and decisions.
- create awareness and knowledge of the gap between current performance and the expected results so that the right suites of solutions can be designed later.
- ensure that people are willing to plan and make needed changes and improvements as well as own the outcomes and results.

AN EXAMPLE OF AN EFFECTIVE APPLICATION OF STANDARD 1

Sally Torrez was assigned to improve the reading performance of students in Grades 7 and 8. She studied the annual test results to determine disaggregated groups of students' current level of performance and their results on interim reading assessments. She observed teachers during their reading instruction and during instruction in other content areas, such as earth science, to see how teachers are teaching reading across the curriculum of the school. She met with the principal to determine what he thinks is working in reading instruction and what could be better. She asked for evidence to support his opinions. She recorded the responses and repeated the interview process with the entire school leadership team, including the instructional coaches who were assigned to develop teachers' teaching skills and groups of teachers by grade level. She compared the responses to the school improvement plan's areas of focus. She reviewed the professional learning records and professional degrees of each teacher (relative to teaching reading). She developed a set of data to represent her findings and observations. Torrez had some hunches about what was happening in the school and how to improve reading, but she decided to let the data tell the story so that those she interviewed and others in the school could first see the self-identified gaps in performance and could agree that the data and observations were valid before beginning to diagnose why the gaps existed or how to close them.

During her inquiry, Torrez studied the Lexile scores of students on reading tests after the first two weeks of school. Since Lexile scores provide a common scale for measuring text difficulty and student reading ability, she knew that reviewing students' data was critical to helping both the teachers who were teaching reading and those teaching other content to inform instructional strategies. She knew that reading must be taught in every classroom and that research pointed to specific interventions that needed to be in place to support reading across the curriculum as well as processes that teachers and instructional coaches could use to determine how well the methods they are trying to help students learn to read well is working. However, her observations led her to believe that teachers in content areas outside language arts were not using the research-based practices that could ensure students were reading at or above the Lexile levels for the texts and supplemental materials used in their classrooms. She also observed that all teachers where not effectively studying whether the interventions they were using with struggling readers were working on a student-by-student basis. However, in each classroom she observed, she both thanked the teacher for allowing her to observe and pointed out any of the appropriate reading instructional practices she saw.

Torrez thought she knew what it would take to bring adoption of research-based reading interventions to scale in both the targeted reading instruction and general classroom instruction; however, she knew that first she had to help teachers see the difference between how their students were performing in reading and how they could be performing and between how they were teaching and how they could be teaching and how well they were assessing students' responses to reading interventions.

She prepared an activity to conduct with teachers, instructional coaches, and administrators to share the data she had collected and engage them in discerning and rating the existing gaps in student and teacher performance.

After Torrez collected the data and constructed an activity to allow teachers, instructional coaches, and administrators to see the current and desired state of reading performance, she called the school principal. "I have done some inquiry in the 7th and 8th grade students' reading performance as well as the reading teaching practices we are using in reading instruction, including in general classrooms. I have some data to share and some observations I have made. Would you like me to share this with you first or with a group you select before I conduct an activity to share it with all the teachers? How would you like to proceed? I want to make sure I am on target with what I think and what others see is happening before we begin to work together to find some solutions."

The principal asked her to brief him, the leadership team, and the special education director on the data and observations. She opened the meeting by assuring the group that she was committed to making them successful in leading improvement of reading and that she was optimistic that the faculty could improve the reading performance of all students, including those who were struggling. Following her presentation, she said to the group, "These are just initial findings based on study of the data, observations, and interviews. Am I on track? I want to make sure I have your input before I share this with the faculty, and of course, I will be seeking their feedback when I present it. It is critical that, together, we help everyone understand that the whole school and its support systems are responsible and able to improve the reading of all the students here."

AN EXAMPLE OF A LESS EFFECTIVE APPLICATION OF STANDARD 1

Xavier Richardson was assigned as a performance coach to improve reading in Grades 7 and 8. He was confident that he could improve reading performance, given his experience teaching reading and his broad and deep research of best practices for improving reading. As he studied the annual reading test scores of students and the initial reading assessment in both grades at the start of the year, he saw both groups of students and individual students who were not reading at Lexile levels appropriate to their age and grade level. He developed a detailed spreadsheet of the student data and analyzed it to determine the students who were underperforming, on track, and performing very well in their reading assessments. Next, he developed a plan for improving their reading performance and asked the principal to allow him to present it at the next faculty meeting.

After Richardson presented the data at the faculty meeting, he said to the group, "I have been fortunate to have been working for several years in teaching and researching practices in improving students' reading performance. Clearly, this school has room for improvement, and I have some practices that I will be helping you adopt to improve students' reading performance. I am now going to review those practices with you so that you will know what the best practices are and what I will be looking for in your classrooms and as you work together. For those of you who teach in content areas that typically do not teach students to read or improve reading, I can show you how to fix this so that all students read at high levels." Richardson then gave a presentation on the practices research had found to be most effective in improving reading. At the conclusion, he said, "I hope all of you now know what I will be looking for as I observe your classrooms over the next couple of weeks. Now I am going to give each of you a schedule for when I will be observing your classroom, and I will write a prescription for each of you concerning practices you should adopt, based on what research says. Do you have any questions?"

Following his observation in each classroom, Richardson developed a set of recommendations for each grade level of what needed to be done to improve reading at each grade level and presented it to the principal along with recommendations to adopt a reading program that he knew was grounded in research-based reading improvement practices. He volunteered to help the principal assist teachers in the adoption of the program and to introduce it along with a summary of the gaps he found in teaching performance at the next faculty meeting.

REFLECTION

1. Compare and contrast what Torrez and Richardson did in their improvement efforts.

2. What did Torrez do that made a positive difference?

3. In your opinion, what could prevent Richardson from making progress with the school team?

4. What in this chapter will be useful to you in your practice of facilitating improvement?

POWER POINTS

Each chapter will include tips, techniques, and guidelines about how to gain and sustain your fluency in facilitating school improvement and help schools transform to meet 21st-century demands. Here are some points based on this chapter:

- Make it a habit to check out the latest research about the factors that support or impede performance, why certain interventions are effective, and what has to be in place for them to be effective. To find useful data, periodically visit the websites of the latest publications and do searches for new ideas and findings that will reinforce your position as an expert. As you begin this work, remember that not everyone values data the same way. Some people make it a point to discount the evidence because it does not support their ideas about what the problem is or their recommended solution. Remember that data without analyses rarely support valid conclusions. Also remember that even though qualitative data measure opinions, they are still valid if there are corroborating data. Opinions matter. All data are just points in time; by themselves, they do not predict or support conclusions.

- Sometimes people may be overwhelmed and need time to digest the initial findings and observations or they may miss arriving at the conclusions that certain changes are needed. If you sense they are not realizing the implications of the findings or are reticent to commit to needed changes, you may say, "It looks like you need some time to study and think about this." Let them know you will be back in touch by a specific date. If you have committed to report to their supervisor, let them know that you must do this and that you would like to have some conclusions agreed upon as soon as possible so that next steps can be planned, and you can report this progress.

- Coming in as a know-it-all or touting your expertise can trigger defensiveness in the people you are assigned to help. It is important to communicate through what you say and do that you are there to listen to and truly hear what they think and feel.

- Go in prepared. Analyze the available performance data in advance, but do not say, "I have seen your data."

- Smile; reinforce that you are there to learn and understand and are not playing "got you" or seeking to place blame.

SUMMARY

The work of Standard 1 is performed both at the beginning of facilitating a school improvement cycle and along the way as more data are collected and analyzed, meaning is created, and conclusions are drawn that impact decisions and actions. Meeting this standard requires expert knowledge of how to access, collect, and use the multiple types of data that must be studied to improve the complex systems of work that impact teaching and student learning and performance. While being a respected and effective performance consultant or school leader requires expert knowledge in the systems of teaching and learning and knowledge of how to determine which high-leverage research-based practices might be applied, it also requires you to play several roles. A key role is that of a facilitator, who knows when and how to interpret and present information, elicit others' reactions, call for commitment, and create and maintain a persona of openness and fairness. The following chapters continue with explanations, tools, and examples of the other standards.

See the end of this book for a complete list of resources and references related to data analyses.

Additional materials and resources related to
The School Improvement Specialist Field Guide
can be found on the companion website.
http://www.corwin.com/sisguide

Facilitate Deriving Meaning and Engagement

2

Bailey Pittman looked at the charts before her. The first stage of her work with the high school had produced enough data and information for her to define the gap between the current levels of performance and the levels of performance the school needed to help every student succeed at high levels. Remembering Frank Perez's advice to avoid giving opinions or becoming prescriptive, she had listened closely during initial dialogue with her sponsor, the school superintendent, and those who worked in the school. Her questioning revealed some interesting information that helped her to shape some hypotheses about why the school was performing at the current levels. But she knew she had to remain unbiased and convince those she was facilitating to take responsibility for making changes that would result in improved performance within the school for both the adults and the students. She sent an e-mail to Perez, summarizing what she had accomplished in the initial phase of the assignment. Perez replied:

It sounds like you have a good start to your consulting assignment. The next phase of the work requires you to apply your good facilitation skills. When the adults in the school begin to see the gap that exists, they often become fearful and anxious. This creates a disequilibrium that is actually helpful in the change process, but you have to help them see that change and improvement are possible and that they can make a difference. If you can engage them in meaningful conversations, focused on the data, then you can guide them toward a clear understanding of what is going on that needs to change and their ability to make that change. I have found that it is not unusual for the adults in the school to not really understand their results or why they are not getting the results they may be working hard to achieve. It is also not uncommon for people who work together daily to not really have the types of professional relationships and working structures that provide opportunity for collaboration, on-the-job learning, or peer-to-peer coaching and inquiry.

If you can work with the superintendent who is sponsoring your work to engage the groups in team-based improvement, you will have created the conditions for a successful intervention.

To be continued . . .

At this point in an improvement process, you have studied the performance data and conducted your own inquiry. You have your own expertise to bring to bear, plus a wealth of research that points to the best practices for improvement. The adults you are working with have agreed that some things need to change and that they want to be better than average or among the best of the best.

STANDARD 2: FACILITATE DERIVING MEANING AND ENGAGEMENT

Next, you will focus on turning school improvement from a spectator sport in which others watch you, the expert, do the work to a collaborative learning-by-doing experience with powerful reflection that leads to new knowledge and new ways of behaving and solving problems together. Standard 2 focuses on how you help those you are guiding to create the mental models they need to willingly learn and work with others to affect needed changes.

Creating Meaning

The first element of Standard 2 is focused on the work you will do at the beginning of an improvement effort (and along the journey) to help others establish mental models that prepare them to engage in inquiry, collaborative learning, and discourse and to work together to close the gap between the current and needed performance and results.

2.1 Help others create meaning from findings, research, and inquiry.

Those who do and support the work of schooling have a great deal of knowledge about their schools and the work they do. The critical work of making meaning requires you to facilitate closing the gap between what others know (or think they know) about their school's performance and the facts of its actual performance. If you can help adults see that what they perceive may not be fully accurate or that what they know is incomplete, you have an opportunity to create curiosity, to help others understand the implications of their actions and care about what happens next.

Like a good teacher, your role will be to engage those you are facilitating by setting a context, building on prior knowledge, and creating new knowledge. An effective school improvement specialist uses a process that allows the work to draw others in and engage them in solving a mystery in which they are the characters, the protagonists. How you lead them through this discovery process will ultimately determine the level of engagement by those who must do the work.

Logic tells you that if those you are guiding knew how to solve the problems that negatively impact their schools, they would do it. They chose this profession because they care about students and want to help them succeed. Common sense tells you that the people you are trying to help are educated, and most are experienced. You know that the vast majority are or have been teachers—the very people who are expected to know the answers and to teach them to others. Add to that the challenge of dealing with the group of individuals who have the hardest time absorbing new ideas: adults.

You may recall that Maria Montessori, the Italian educator for whom the Montessori Method of teaching and learning is named, defined the mind of a young child as able to gain knowledge quickly and effortlessly, using what she called the *absorbent mind* (Haines, 1993). Following Montessori's logic, the adult mind has been absorbing knowledge for a long time, becoming a sponge soaked with prior knowledge. Adults sift and sort new knowledge against their prior knowledge, deciding what to accept and reject. This means the minds of the people you are helping have knowledge and experiences that guide their actions and decisions. Your task is to get them to be willing and able to absorb new information that is needed for future actions and decisions. By helping them recognize the gap between what they think they know and what actually exists, you will create the conditions to engage them in the work that will bring about needed improvements.

If the adults you are working with think they know everything about their school, students, and performance, you will have to work diligently to combat their overconfidence and gently make the gap between what they know and need to know apparent. This process of engaging adults in school improvement may be similar to the process many teachers use to pique students' interest by using *Advance Organizers*, as shown in Figure 2.1. The group you are working with will fill in what they know and what they are learning as they work together. As their inquiry unfolds, they will be able to identify what else they need to know.

Alternatively, you may give them information in a story format that tempts them to become curious and propels them to learn and act in new ways. It is important that you carefully plan the sequencing of the information they will study, as opposed to bombarding them with

Figure 2.1   Advance Organizer

What I Know	What I Am Learning	What I Need to Know

massive amounts of information all at once. A successful process involves giving them clues by asking the right questions, building awareness of their knowledge gaps, and guiding them to collaboratively untangle the ill-structured problem of an underperforming school.

An effective way to help others create meaning from the available data is to bring together a group you are facilitating and ask every member of the group to make individual predictions about school performance, based on what they already know. Ideally, you want to structure this so they see that not everyone agrees with all of the predictions. Oddly enough, bringing to light disagreements about the right answers and helping adults see gaps between their opinions and the opinions of others are steps to creating consensus later. For example, when choosing the facts you want investigated and understood, you might say something like, "I have a series of predictions for you to make. I will give you the questions and allow you time to come up with your predictions, based on what you know. Then each of you will share your predictions with the group and compare them."

Consider this sample prediction activity:

There are 347 students in first grade. Given our current graduation and student achievement rates, when this cohort of students reaches graduation age

- what percentage will graduate?
- what percentage will read at a 12th-grade level?
- how many will have the math skills needed to succeed as freshman in either a four-year college or technical college math class?
- how many will graduate from high school with both an academic diploma and a certification in skills required for the jobs they will need to be able to have a desirable quality of life?
- of those who do not graduate, what percentage is likely to be incarcerated in their lifetime?
- what three things under the control of the school will have happened over their school experience to increase the odds that every student will be ready for postsecondary learning and work?

This process strips away the theories, the excuses, and the preconceptions that might already exist and focuses on the facts and possibilities.

A prediction activity like this requires computation, application of what is known to what is unknown, and often, admission that more data or information is needed. By raising the unexpected idea that people might be working on solutions without all the information, you create curiosity. By allowing each adult to see that some people agree with his or her predictions and understandings and some do not, you can move them collectively forward. In essence, you are saying, "So here is what you say you know and expect . . . Now here is what you are missing, what is needed to solve this puzzle. . . . How can we learn more to inform our work?"

Another process for creating meaning is to "place a face on failure." You can do this by displaying a slide from a page of a yearbook or other composite photos of at least ten students whose demographics reflect the student population, perhaps from a first-grade class. Ask those you are facilitating to make their predictions about how many of those students will drop out of school, based on the current dropout rate. Next, reveal the answers by dimming the photos of the students who would not reach the performance target, applying the current performance data you have collected. For example, if the on-time graduation rate is 85 percent, eliminate 15 percent of the students' photos. This allows you to make the facts known in a way that avoids talking *at* those you are helping. It also allows you to engage the adults you are working with in focusing on the fate of those children who do not meet the targets, which then allows these adults to connect emotionally to the cause. This moves the conversation from analyzing faceless data to solving real problems that impact real lives and the community in which these educators and other stakeholders live. Rather than leading them to envision plodding along a long hard path to improvement, you give a sudden and dramatic glimpse of how the students' lives and the needed improvements can unfold and then engage them as authors of that vision.

Exercises like this help others create meaning and recognize gaps. Once you have helped them wring out their sponges a bit, fueled their curiosity, and convinced them that their work will make a difference, you are ready to help others do their own inquiry and research. As mentioned in Chapter 1, you should avoid the seductive trap of telling them the improvement needs and possible causes or solutions. Instead, facilitate their inquiry by helping them recognize where they are now and then guiding them in analyzing data and identifying the practices, or what they are doing now, that have led to the current situation.

Identifying Systemic Performance Factors

Now is the time to introduce the notion of *performance factors*, those issues in the work, workers, and workplace that impact the performance of the adults who work in schools and the performance of the students they serve, teach, and lead. Although it is too early to begin true cause analysis, engaging them in identifying the wide range of systemic factors that impact performance can help them recognize the link between what is happening in the school, what they and others are doing, and the results achieved. The *Performance Factors Analysis Worksheet* (Tool 2.1) can help you do this work.

Tool 2.1 Performance Factors Analysis Worksheet

Guidelines: This worksheet is meant to help you capture the group's beliefs about what is impacting performance and to focus their attention on a broad range of factors so they can identify all the drivers of performance that must be addressed. You can display each section of the worksheet on a white board or flipchart or project it from a computer. The information you collect will help you build on what you have learned in your initial independent inquiry, using the tools described in Chapter 1. When asking the group to respond, take steps to ensure that everyone contributes. Be sure to share and compare the data and findings from your research after they answer each question.

Section I: Results—the desired outcomes and outputs; performance targets

1. What results need to improve?

2. How do you know that they need improvement?

Section II: The Work—the activities adults must do in schools to produce the outcomes and results of the school

1. What *work* of adults in the school (or school district) impacts the outcomes and results that need to improve?

2. What is impacting the effectiveness, quality, and value of the *work* of adults in the school (or school district) that is *within* the control of the adults in the school or school district? How do you know these factors are impacting the adults' work?

3. What is impacting the effectiveness, quality, and value of the *work* of the adults in the school (or school district) that is *outside* the control of the adults in the school or school district

and which must be managed? How do you know these factors are impacting the adults' work?

Section III: The Workplace—the situation in which the work of *education* occurs within the school and/or school district

1. What within the *workplace* impacts the adults' work and its results? (Consider the culture, job or work design, leadership, supervision, organizational design, available support, time, resources, staffing, teamwork, rewards and sanctions, alignment, and so on.) How do you know that this is an impacting factor?

2. Of those *workplace* factors, which are in control of the adults who work in the school or who support the work of the school? Which are out of their control (that they must over-come or respond to in order to do their work effectively and get the needed results)?

Section IV: The Workers—the adults who work within the school or school district whose performance impacts the outcomes and results

1. Do all *workers* have the knowledge or skills required to achieve the results? What (if any) knowledge and skills need to be enhanced? For whom? How do you know?

2. Are the *workers* motivated to do what needs to be done? What increases or impairs motivation to achieve the right results? What would encourage the right behaviors? How do you know? Does every worker know what is expected? How are expectations set and communicated? How is individual performance inspected and evaluated? What happens when a worker is not meeting expectations?

3. Are the *workers* individually able to achieve success? Are the workers able to perform their work with the degree of skill and collaboration needed to achieve success? How do you know this?

4. What are you personally in control of that could make it possible to achieve the needed improvements and results?

5. What actions produce results that currently *exceed* what is required?

6. What actions contribute to a failure to produce the desired result?

Categorizing Performance Factors

Once the group has created a list of systemic performance factors, you can support making meaning of all they have discussed by using the *Factor Diagram Guidelines* (Tool 2.2). A factor diagram is a simple tool used to help groups organize variables. The tool is

- useful for bringing additional issues or variables to the surface.
- effective for organizing a large number of issues or variables.
- designed to encourage creative thinking and to break down communication barriers.
- meant to be done live and in-person with everyone in the same room at the same time.
- useful for grouping related sets of variables for further inquiry.

Later, you can use the categories created during the factor diagrams activity when doing cause analysis. However, before you dig into the causes, it is important to establish understandings and agreements

---

Tool 2.2   Factor Diagram Guidelines

Guidelines: Follow these steps to create a factor diagram to organize the performance factors the group believes are important to address in the work ahead.

1. Ask the group, "What group of performance factors should we focus upon first: the work, workplace, or workers?'"

2. Ask the individuals to write down all the factors identified in the chosen category, such as all the workplace factors, putting each one on a separate sticky note.*

3. Post all notes on a common surface.

4. Lead the group in organizing the notes into broad categories, placing related responses together, striking duplications, and labeling the categories.

5. Ask the group, "What factors have we overlooked that need to be added?"

6. Discuss the results. Ask "If this is what is impacting our results, what are the implications for the improvement work ahead for this group?"

*Save time by recording each factor in the initial *Performance Factors Analysis* (Tool 2.1) on a separate sticky note.

regarding the implications of group members' current and future actions and decisions. These agreements will help to build shared commitment to encouraging the behaviors driving required changes.

Comprehending Implications

It is critical that you lead this exploration and inquiry with individuals who by working together and engaging others can make the needed changes, adopt new behaviors, and improve practices. Handled appropriately, you can convince them, both individually and collectively, of their responsibility and ability to bring about improvements. Focus on what is within the group's control to change and what they cannot change (but must account for) so that they stay focused on the right work.

> Focus on what is within the group's control to change and what they cannot change (but must account for) so that they stay focused on the right work.

The performance factors analysis you lead lays important groundwork for achieving the next element of Standard 2:

2.2 Help others comprehend the implications of their actions, recognize patterns, and accept new responsibilities.

Next, your role is to help those you are supporting to link what they identified as gaps in performance and the related performance factors to the behaviors, actions, or decisions of the people who can affect needed changes, including themselves. This process is not about placing blame or pointing out past mistakes but about identifying who can make a difference.

Tool 2.3, the *Improvement Ownership Worksheet*, can help define who needs to be involved in the next stages of inquiry to address each performance factor. Use one worksheet for each performance factor or category of performance factor. For example, a category could be "resources," while a single performance factor in the category might be "time for collaborative planning." Note: the task is not to propose solutions but to identify (1) who in the group has ownership and can act to affect change, (2) who outside the group can help by their actions and decisions, and (3) what factors cannot be changed (such a loss of funding) but must be responded to or worked around to close a performance gap. The results of this analysis can also help the group identify patterns and trends that add meaning to their inquiry.

After the group has defined the performance factors and determined who outside the group to engage, it is time to form improvement teams to collaboratively study the causes and develop solutions.

Tool 2.3   Improvement Ownership Worksheet

Guidelines: Identify the factors the group needs to address, and facilitate the group through the process of completing the form. Once it is complete, ask the group the following questions:

1. What patterns or trends do we see emerging from our inquiry to date?

2. What must be done to organize ourselves and others to further study and address those trends and patterns?

Performance Factor to Address	Who in our group can affect change by their behavior or decisions?	Who outside our group is needed to affect change by their behavior or decisions?	If the factor cannot be changed, who is in a position to help work around it or respond to it to achieve the needed results?

Building Supportive Relationships

The third element of Standard 2 focuses on nurturing collaborative team-based improvement by facilitating structured, effective communication within the group and with others outside the group who can support or make needed changes.

> 2.3 Build supportive relationships among stakeholders by initiating and sustaining dialogue between individuals and groups.

The *Improvement Team Purpose Worksheet* (Tool 2.4) can help the group clarify for itself what the work ahead entails and who will be involved.

You can use it to draft and share the charter or purpose each improvement team is to meet by working collaboratively on a project or set of projects together over a specific time span. Help those you are guiding to recognize that at this point, they are not yet putting forth solutions but are engaging the right people in teams to do the work that needs to be done to achieve better results.

After the charters or purposes for each targeted improvement team have been developed, it is time to draft the teams. You must talk to the person who is sponsoring the improvement efforts about the proposed memberships of each team. Once the teams have been approved, use Tool 2.5, the *Team Launch Guidelines*, to work with the sponsor to communicate to team members' supervisors.

Tool 2.4   Improvement Team Purpose Worksheet

Guidelines: Guide the group in defining the purpose of each improvement team that will be formed to address specific performance gaps and in determining who each team's members will be, who will sponsor the work, what the deliverables will be, and what the timeline for completion will be. This tool also supports an ongoing discussion about the makeup of the group.

Purpose of this improvement team:
Members:
Sponsor(s):
Deliverables and timelines:

Tool 2.5   Team Launch Guidelines

Guidelines: Discuss the following list of items with the sponsor and supervisors. Help them develop appropriate responses concerning the following:

1. the purpose of the team to which the team members have been assigned
2. why they are important to the team to which they have been assigned
3. what is expected of them
4. the time that will be required and the schedules and deadlines
5. the authority and responsibility the team has
6. the expectation for teams to set and follow norms
7. who will be leading each team

Ask for each supervisor to commit to supporting each team member's work on the improvement project. Typically, this requires the supervisor to arrange work schedules or assignments so that each individual can participate without negatively impacting teaching and learning or other assigned duties.

Once the supervisors of team members have approved those individuals' participation, you are ready to conduct the improvement team launch. Invite the team members to the kickoff meeting and use the *Team Launch Guidelines* to communicate what they need to know to begin their work.

Establishing Norms

Once improvement teams are formed and charged with responsibility for improvement, help them develop a list of *norms* or ground rules for how those working in each team will interact. Norms need not be complicated and may be as simple as "Treat each other with respect," "Arrive and end on time," or "Everyone has an equal voice." It may be useful to post agreed-upon norms in the meeting room or to include them on every agenda.

The most effective norms are those that have been created by the group to manage their own behavior. Provide examples of norms for your group, and then guide them to create a list that meets their needs and expectations. The following is a sample set of norms developed by Penny Smith, a Certified School Improvement Specialist, with a group she has facilitated to improve high school performance:

- Honor every participant's value and knowledge.
- Enjoy and contribute to our learning experiences.
- Engage fully in all workshop learning activities, including networking.
- Be present, on time, and on task.
- Complete all assignments and activities.
- Set cell phones to silent or vibrate.
- Remain in the meeting room during group work. (P. Smith, personal communication, August 20, 2011)

Developing Agendas

Having predefined structures for group meetings helps keep everyone on track and provides order and clarity for how group time will be spent.

Tool 2.6   Agenda Template

Guidelines: This template is meant to help you quickly put together an agenda for your group's working sessions. Formalizing the agendas will help you maintain a document trail of who was involved, what occurred, and when it happened.

Meeting title:

Date:

Time: from _____

To _____

Meeting called by:

Attendees:

Please read in advance:

Please bring these supplies:

Time From: To:	Topic or Task By Whom?	Where? (If One Meeting Occurs in Several Locations)
From: To:	Topic or task: By whom?	Where?
From: To:	Topic or task: By whom?	Where?
From: To:	Topic or task: By whom?	Where?

Deliverables to be achieved during this meeting:

Next steps, directions, and deadlines:

Decisions made:

You should develop agendas for each group meeting and help groups commit to the habit of using agendas when you are not involved. Include the deliverables to be produced by the end of the meeting (outputs, plans, decisions, etc.). The simple *Agenda Template* (Tool 2.6) can help you prepare for effective meetings.

After your groups are organized to take the next steps to close performance gaps, help them to understand and agree upon (in advance) how decisions are to be made. It may be necessary to discuss the options for decision making with them or to train them in group decision-making processes.

Facilitating Group Communication

One of your responsibilities is to conduct meetings in ways that reduce the influence of overly powerful group members. A key aspect of building supportive relationships is not letting the group defer to the opinions of those who are in higher positions of authority, carry high levels of informal influence, or who are more vocal in their opinions. One technique is to purposefully assign parts of the agenda to those with less power of position. Another approach when facilitating discussions is to use Tool 2.7, the *Modified Nominal Group Technique.* This process lets the group know that you will call on everyone; then do so in either a random order or in a sequence where the more influential members are called on last. Do not use an open call, such as "Who would like to comment on this?"

Tool 2.7   Modified Nominal Group Technique

Guidelines: This process is very effective at controlling group dynamics, especially in making sure everyone believes his or her opinion was considered.

1. Ask or post a question.

2. Ask the group to privately generate a list of short responses. Ideally, every response is a short noun-verb phrase. You do not want long answers.

3. In a round robin format, ask each member to share one response until everyone has shared one answer to the question.

Tell the group that there will be time to discuss and comment on what is shared later in the process. Remember to number the responses.

4. Repeat the round robin until everyone has exhausted his or her list of answers to the question. With each round, you can start with another person.

5. Discuss responses. Ask the group if they want to ask questions about any of the responses or make any comments.

6. Combine and eliminate responses. Ask the group if they see ways to reduce the number of responses because they are redundant. However, do not eliminate or alter a response unless you have permission from the person who generated it.

7. Rank the top five responses. Ask the group to privately pick the top five responses from the complete list.

8. Assign values to top five. Once everyone has picked their top five responses, ask them to assign values—5 points to the most important (critical), 4 points to the next, 3 to the next, 2 to the next, and 1 to the least important. Do not allow them to assign percentages or fractions. You want whole numbers. If you want, you can determine if there is a statistically significant difference for the responses receiving the highest points. You do this by computing the average and standard deviation. Responses one or more standards deviations above the average are statistically significant.

9. Attach values to the responses. Go down the list of responses one by one and ask if anyone assigned points to it. Record the total number of points assigned to each response.

10. Discuss the results. Comment on which responses received the highest number of points. Comment on the degree to which the group is in agreement on the importance of the factors (note that the number of responses that were assigned points is a measure of consensus). Comment on any similarities in the responses selected.

11. Proceed to the next question. Repeat the process if there are other questions.

Building Commitment

The fourth element of Standard 2 is about building commitment.

2.4 Develop commitment so that people act in new ways, feel engaged, and believe that change is possible.

At this point in setting the stage for collaborative improvement efforts, you have facilitated the group in agreeing on the need for change, the factors that impact results, and who can affect change and in adopting standardized structures and processes for communicating and working together. Next, you will engage them in setting priorities. Tool 2.8, The *Performance Gap and Priority Matrix,* can help you guide your group through the process of agreeing on which gaps in performance to address and the priorities for closing those gaps, based on criticality. Using this tool can help those you are supporting to lead the change, to take a broad look at all the improvement needs, and, after considering who needs to be involved, to ensure that team-based improvement projects can be effectively coordinated, resourced, and carried out without placing too much work on any one group or set of individuals.

Tool 2.8   The Performance Gap and Priority Matrix

Guidelines: List the factors the group wants to take into consideration when deciding on criticality, and rate each from high to low. When using this tool, you may help the group consider for each performance factor the number of students impacted, the number of teacher impacted, the availability of funding, the impact on other efforts, or other variables.

Performance Gaps Generate this list individually, then repeat as a group and reach consensus on ratings.	1	2	3	4	5	6	7	8

If the group or groups you are facilitating can reach agreements on gaps, factors, and priorities, it is time to seal the deal. This can be done through shared commitments and the creation of intrinsic motivators, such as an appropriate degree of autonomy so the group can research the causes of gaps, study the research-based interventions that could be applied to address or mitigate the impact of those causes, and close the gaps. According to the Gallup Organization's research, the opportunity for members to contribute their unique strengths and talents at the appropriate time can be a strong motivator. Providing them a chance to be a part of a winning team or to master new skills will add value to the organization and to each person's career (Buckingham & Coffman, 1999).

Using Stories

To help teams be effective, it is important that the members know each other and what each contributes. It would seem that the people on each improvement team would know the strengths of their colleagues and what value each brings to the team; however, in a context where a true culture of collaborative teaching and learning has not been established, it is not unusual that team members know little about each other in a professional sense. Engaging the team members in an activity that can bring this information to light before they begin seeking solutions can help create understandings that support change and collaboration. The process will also give you valuable insights into beliefs, capabilities, and strengths that can be leveraged as well as organizational issues that will impact your ability to facilitate change and improvement.

There are those who see this type of school improvement facilitation work as "fluff" because it deals with the social and emotional aspect of school improvement, but by taking the time to guide the individuals you are working with through these activities, you can reveal what each person

- can and is willing to contribute to the improvement effort.
- believes he or she does best.
- is willing to learn or do that is new or different.
- is motivated by so that you can help them to choose their role and remain in it.
- believes about teaching and learning.
- has identified as strengths and positives that can be leveraged.

If you can help those you are guiding to share their successes, beliefs, strengths, and best intentions, you can create a context in which people believe they can do the work ahead together, because they have evidence of success in the past and recognize the intangible value that each person brings to the team. Guiding them to reflect upon and express their strengths, passions, and hopes for the future can create a climate and bond for making a difference, even when the work ahead seems difficult. You can use Tool 2.9, the *My Story Guide*, to engage those who will be working together to affect change to better understand what each person brings to the table for the good of the group's shared work as well as their individual and collective visions for a more positive future after changes are made.

Tool 2.9   My Story Guide

Guidelines: Emphasize that this activity is a freewriting experience, so those participating should not be concerned with the technical aspects of writing, such as sentence structure or punctuation. The goal is to let their thoughts flow onto their paper as they reflect on the question or idea. Let them know that they will later share their reflections, but no one else will read their writings. Provide the group with protected time to respond to the questions below.

1. What inspired you to become an educator?

2. What attracted you to your role in this school?

3. What has been a high point in your experience here?

4. What beliefs guide your day-to-day actions and decisions as you work with students and other adults in this school?

5. What knowledge, skills, expertise, or resources do you bring to the improvement efforts ahead?

6. What level of time and attention are you willing and able to devote to this project?

7. If you had three wishes for this school that would come true if expressed in positive terms, what would they be?

After the group members have finished this writing activity, arrange a time for them to meet in small groups and share what they have written. If needed, organize the groups so that the people who will most need to collaborate during the improvement effort share this experience. Reintroduce the norms the group has established and lead the sharing so that every member is heard. It is important to keep the conversation positive.

If in the sharing process a negative or problem is stated, redirect the speaker by asking a question like, "I hear you saying you wish that issue was different. Assume the issue was addressed and you witnessed the best outcome you could imagine, what would that look like from your point of view?" This approach can maintain positive dialogue and put the responsibility on the group member to imagine how something can be changed and improved, rather than focusing on barriers and problems as insurmountable.

The compilation of these statements can be shaped into a compelling document that captures the progress of the group and provides a point-in-time snapshot of what the group is drawing on as it begins solution-seeking. As the facilitator of improvement, it is critical that you collect the artifacts of your facilitation along the way to support your evaluation efforts later and to document your practices and proficiency.

Gaining Commitments

It is also important that you communicate your beliefs that the group or groups can work together to close the gaps and that you are committed to their success. The *Commitments and Contributions Worksheet* (Tool 2.10) can help you facilitate the agreements you and the group members need to make individually and collectively to guide actions and decisions. The purpose of this tool is to elicit public commitments from the group members and to generate ideas about what the group will accept as evidence that a commitment has been honored. You can recreate the form on an electronic white board or display it from your computer. However it is displayed, you will want to generate a document that includes this information so you and the group can reference it later. You may also want to pose the results on the group's blog or other shared workspace.

Your facilitation of commitment-building processes also provides a positive model for others. Remember, it is not necessary to change people's beliefs before beginning improvement efforts. Many adults initially doubt ideas that challenge their beliefs; however, you can facilitate adults into new ways of acting that change their beliefs over time.

Tool 2.10   Commitments and Contributions Worksheet

Guidelines: This tool helps a group discuss what level of commitment they are willing to make and what they and others will accept as evidence of commitment.

I am committed to contribute the following to our shared commitment to closing the performance gaps we have identified:	The following evidence will prove these commitments:

Signature: _____

Date: _____

AN EXAMPLE OF AN EFFECTIVE APPLICATION OF STANDARD 2

Dr. Mary Ann Brown was assigned to facilitate the improvement of Fields Elementary School, situated in a community that had transitioned in three years from being relatively affluent to having a bimodal population of students from middle-class families and from families living at or below the poverty level. At the same time, the population had shifted from being nearly equally white and African American to being very diverse, representing at least 30 different nationalities. The school has slipped from being one of the top-performing schools in the school district to performing at or below the district average in most grades and subject areas. Most of the faculty, staff, and administrators worked in the school for several years, but 20 percent of the teachers had less than three years of teaching experience due to retirements by the veteran faculty.

When given the assignment, she was told that she was charged with helping the team understand what needed to change and how to make those changes happen. Brown was provided the school's performance data, the school improvement plan, budget, personnel information, and three years of annual reports on the school. She was reminded that Dr. Stacy Francis had been assigned to work with the school last year and had quit at the end of the school year due to frustration over the lack of progress with the faculty and administrators who clung to the belief that they were a very good school until the community changed and that they were not responsible for the challenges that change created.

Brown knew that changing those beliefs was central to facilitating success for the adults and students in the school and that the school year ahead was going to be a learning experience for everyone involved. She focused first on helping the school's internal stakeholders come to their own conclusions that change was needed. She thoroughly reviewed all the data and information provided and identified groups of students who were underperforming compared to their peers. She then identified the teachers who were assigned those students for the coming year. Over the next six weeks, she collected data, interviewed faculty administrators, and listened to their ideas, beliefs, and concerns. She worked hard to build professional trust and to demonstrate that she was seeking to understand the problems, without preconceived ideas regarding solutions. She visited classrooms daily, observing instruction and expressing appreciation to each teacher for the opportunity to observe. The overwhelming sentiment of those she interviewed and observed was that they were working hard and doing their best for their students.

After collecting other information and data, Brown collected the results of the first round of benchmark exams, student assessments conducted at the end of each sixth week. Before the teachers reviewed the students' results, Brown scheduled a series of working sessions with groups of teachers. She instructed each teacher to bring two duplicate copies of the class roster for each group of students taught.

Brown began the session by thanking the teachers for bringing their class rosters. She reminded them that they would later share the results of their students' six-week benchmark exams. She provided colored highlighter pens and asked the teacher to predict how each student would perform on the benchmark exam, based on the first six weeks of teaching and learning. Students who they predicted would score below the standard were to be marked with an orange marker. Students who they thought would score about average were marked with a yellow marker, and students who they predicted would perform the best were marked with a green marker.

After the predictions were marked, Brown informed the teachers that their students' performance data from last year were summarized on charts in alphabetical order on the rear wall of the meeting room. She asked each teacher to find each student on their roster and compare whether or not their predictions for each student were consistent with that student's performance last year. They were asked to place a check mark by every prediction they made that matched last year's performance.

After the teachers reviewed the performance data against their own predictions, she reassembled the group and asked them to share any insights they had gained. As the teachers debriefed, a discovery emerged: The majority of their predictions did not match last year's actual performance by each student.

Brown then passed out the results for each class from the first six-week benchmark exams. She asked the teachers to take their second roster and to highlight, using the same color system, the actual performance of each student on the interim benchmark exam. She then asked the group to compare their students' actual performance to what they expected. Another discovery emerged: Students were performing very close to what the teacher expected on the benchmark exam. Brown asked the group to put forward hypotheses as to why their predictions did not as closely match last year's performance but were close to how students actually performed on the benchmark exam.

Through their discussion, teachers expressed their hypotheses, and Brown provided them with additional reports that the teachers could use to identify which groups of students were struggling and which were performing well, based on last year's data and the first six weeks' data. After their data review and realization of the match or gap between their expectations and student performance, the group members shared their insights. The common understanding was that what they believed students could do was impacting what their students were achieving. Brown then facilitated the teachers in using last year's data and the first six weeks of data for this year to identify students who needed extra support (including acceleration) and those students who were meeting standards but that could be challenged to exceed the standards, thus increasing rigor for all. She closed the meeting by asking the group to begin thinking of the barriers that needed to be overcome in order to help every student improve their performance and to be ready to report on these barriers at the next meeting. She e-mailed a *Performance Factors Analysis Worksheet* to every member of the group to use to collect their thoughts, data, and evidence.

In the follow-up meeting, Brown helped the groups to set norms for their work ahead together and shared the agenda for the session. She then facilitated groups through a review of their performance factors analysis. She recorded their findings using an electronic whiteboard in the teachers' work room. She then used the *Modified Nominal Group Technique* to guide the groups in prioritizing the top three issues that they believed needed to be studied further. After the meeting, she e-mailed a short report to each group member with a link to a blog she had created for the group members. Brown asked each to respond on the blog with their opinions of what performance gaps needed to be closed, using the same group norms established for in-person meetings.

Brown monitored the blog and compiled the gaps that had been identified using a performance gaps and priority matrix. Behind the scenes, she worked with the principal to create protected time each week for the groups to meet. Gradually, she noticed that the quality of ideas and the amount of input on the blog had increased.

A few days later, Brown sent each group member the performance gaps and priority matrix she had compiled as an electronic survey. She asked the group members to individually prioritize the gaps they had identified. She collected the survey results and produced a report that showed their collective ranking of the gaps in priority order. Brown sent out the report along with a notice for the next group meeting and an agenda. She asked for continued input via the blog and monitored the responses.

During the next meeting with the group, she reviewed the prioritized gaps and told them, "It seems that we have agreement on some specific gaps to be closed. Before we start deeper analysis of the causes of these gaps, I want to facilitate an activity that will help us identify what you individually and collectively can bring to the table to close these gaps. There is a great deal of talent and expertise in this group, and I fully expect and believe that you will succeed in closing the performance gaps before us. I am going to give you some protected time to answer a short set of questions."

Brown passed out the *My Story Guide* for the freewriting exercise and gave the group members the rest of the meeting time to answer the questions. She then said, "Our time is up for today. Please take the questions with you and add anything that comes to mind through the week. We will meet the same time next week, and please bring your responses with you. Of course, if you want to share any of your responses, you are welcome to post them on the blog." She reminded the group members of the norms that had been established for their meetings and blogs.

The next week, Brown said, "I did not develop a formal agenda for today, because we only have one thing to do and that is share your thoughts and ideas from the questions you answered." She facilitated the group as they shared for about 45 minutes, stopping to redirect problem statements to expressions of possibility. She recorded their discussions and promised to post them to the blog.

"We have revealed a great many strengths, talents, and positive possibilities today," she said. "I will be e-mailing each of you a *Contributions and Commitments Worksheet*. Each of you now has a personal page on the internal website. Please fill out the worksheet and post it on your page by Friday, and bring a copy to next week's meeting."

Brown reviewed the website postings and blog comments. She was pleased to find the conversations had shifted from problems to possibilities and that team members openly expressed commitments to contribute to the improvement efforts.

AN EXAMPLE OF A LESS EFFECTIVE APPLICATION OF STANDARD 2

You may recall that Dr. Stacy Francis had been assigned to Fields Elementary School but resigned in frustration after just one year. When she participated in her exit conference, her frustration was evident. "I showed the faculty, staff, and administrators what was not working in the school and what they needed to do to fix it. I pulled all their students' performance data for them and gave them sets of recommendations for the ways to improve what was broken. It seemed obvious to me, given what the data revealed and what the research says has to be done to improve a school like this. It seemed in every meeting that they were on the defensive; they didn't seem to want to take responsibility for making the changes and insisted they were doing all they could do.

I went into every classroom and office and gave them the data I had analyzed. They seemed appreciative, but they also seemed to just stick it in a drawer and not do much with it. I have never seen a group of people who were so resistant to change. In their minds, these students are all performing about as well as they expect them to perform."

REFLECTION

Compare and contrast the approaches of Brown and Francis used in facilitating change.

1. What did Brown do that made a positive difference?

2. In your opinion, what prevented Francis from making more progress with the school team?

3. What in this chapter will be useful to you in your practice of facilitating improvement?

POWER POINTS

Here are some suggestions about how to get the greatest benefit from the ideas in this chapter:

- Learn how to influence groups without them experiencing it as being manipulative. The only difference in influence and manipulation is your intent; therefore, it is critical for your actions and communication to reflect your sincere intention to help others be successful.
- People want to be productive, so you must ask use the right questions and provide sufficient structure that allow them to be efficient, productive, and successful.
- Recognize people's need to know where they stand in relation to others. People may not like hierarchies, yet they are more comfortable when they know where they rank. In education in particular, there is an unstated hierarchy or power structure based on a combination of job title, degrees, and seniority.
- Build trust so that people will be willing to take risks, challenge opinions, ask for evidence, and pose alternative interpretations to the information at hand.
- Create a safe environment that nurtures relationships and protect all of the group's members from unwarranted criticism or disrespect.
- Practice using the tools in this chapter to create meaning and engagement.

SUMMARY

This chapter builds on the ideas presented in Chapter 1. The facilitation skills required to do the work in Chapter 2 may be difficult and subtle, but they can be mastered. The process of helping people to comprehend the meaning and implications of what has been done and what they must do to improve schools and school systems begins with and depends on engagement. Engagement happens when you genuinely listen, solicit opinions, encourage reflection, and point out disparities. The ideas and tools in this chapter including identifying performance factors, exploring the implications of possible actions, taking the risks required to earn the respect and cooperation of others, and publicly making the commitments required for change. By recognizing improvement as a process and purposefully using the tools in this chapter, you can move people to action.

See the end of the book for a complete list of resources and references related to interpreting data and engaging others.

Additional materials and resources related to
The School Improvement Specialist Field Guide
can be found on the companion website.
http://www.corwin.com/sisguide

Focus on Systemic Factors   3

Bailey Pittman was eager to report her progress to Frank Perez. She had facili-
tated sessions with teams that represented all the adults who impacted student
achievement. "After I helped them see the gap in their students' performance, they
began to engage in dialogue about the current state of performance and the desired
state. From their conversations, I could tell that they had not looked at enough
data together to get a clear understanding of their students' results in comparison
with similar schools. I knew we had made a breakthrough when I began to hear
them saying, 'This isn't good enough. Our students can do better, and we want to
help them be better than average. We think our schools are good schools, but we
have the opportunity to make them the best schools. We just need time to work
together.' When I heard that, I knew we were ready to dig deeper. In the past, I have
had a gut sense of what was needed to be done since I knew my school so well, but
I am beginning to see that my role is to get them to come to the right conclusions
of what needs to be done and make the right decisions. What should I do next?"

Frank replied, "It sounds like you are making good progress with the groups
you are facilitating. The next steps build on what you have done so far. If you guide
them into a deeper performance analysis, they can determine all the factors that
are impeding their schools from achieving the results they have targeted. Once they
have a clear understanding of those performance factors, they will need to analyze
the causes of those barriers and factors and determine all the interventions needed
to move from where they are now to where they want to be."

"This step can be a bit tricky," he advised, "because it requires analyzing the
three core systems of the school that those who work in the school know best: cur-
riculum, assessment, and instruction. It also requires analyzing the ancillary sys-
tems and processes that impact student performance, such as teacher assignment,
school schedules, and evaluation."

"Even transportation can impact student outcomes," Frank pointed out. "The
school I am working with now had a problem with on-time arrival of students to
school. Because many of the students eat breakfast at school, if they arrive late and
go to the cafeteria for breakfast, they are late for their first class or subject, which
usually is math or language arts. They are repeatedly missing instruction in key

areas. I found that guiding the adults to identify and analyze the factors, like bus schedules that cause students to be late, can be challenging, but it is necessary to solve the problem and produce sustainable change and improvement."

"I see what you are saying about the challenge of getting people to look across all the performance factors before developing the right interventions," Bailey said. "During my analysis sessions, people were already suggesting solutions. I know I am going to have to help them look at all the performance factors before choosing interventions. Also, I need to help them focus on the higher-level skills students need. There is so much potential here, and I want to help them see what other schools are doing to ensure their students are ready for postsecondary academics and the world of work."

To be continued . . .

Schools are complex organizations operating within ever-changing contexts. Student learning occurs as a result of their experiences with teachers, classmates, school leaders, and family and community members. Teacher and school leader performance is shaped by experiences with colleagues, students, families, and community members. In order to identify and address the factors that stand between what is happening now and the future results you and those you are working with have envisioned, you will guide the team through three processes:

Performance Analysis—uncovering the multiple perspectives about the current situation to identify what is required for people to perform to the expected levels

Cause Analysis—investigating and finding the true reasons for underperformance and the barriers to reaching higher levels of performance

Intervention Selection—studying and selecting the most suitable combination of performance interventions that increase the odds people can and will perform to the expected levels

These processes appear to be discrete, but they are not. Instead, you will discover that although you will start with the performance analysis and then move on to cause analysis and intervention selection, you are likely to revisit your past work. The processes of identifying causes and selecting interventions will bring to the surface the need to further validate what is going on now. As you facilitate the group's discovery, think of it as an adventure, during which you will uncover new findings and insights with each step. By focusing the processes systemically on the *work*, the *workers*, and the *workplace*, you increase the likelihood of uncovering and addressing the real barriers to change and improvement.

> By focusing the processes systemically on the *work*, the *workers*, and the *workplace*, you increase the likelihood of uncovering and addressing the real barriers to change and improvement.

STANDARD 3: FOCUS ON SYSTEMIC FACTORS

Your effectiveness as a facilitator will ultimately be determined by your group's ability to understand the current state, to accurately identify the factors that are preventing the desired performance, and to choose sustainable improvements that not only solve current problems but advance students toward mastery of 21st-century skills. Therefore, as you study the host of factors that are impacting the current performance of students, teachers, administrators, and leaders, you must maintain a future focus that continually challenges the group to define what students will need to perform to meet standards and to master the skills needed to be successful in the future.

For example, if the group you are helping has identified and decided to study and close a gap in math scores for a student group that is not meeting standards, your role is to help them use math content standards to influence selection of (1) interventions that could support those students to meet the standards and (2) interventions that could help those students exceed the standards and develop the types of skills they will need to be successful in the 21st century.

As you guide the group to select interventions, ask them to clarify the goal. Is the goal to help students recall formulas for passing the test, or is the goal to engage the students in using the formulas to be able to solve real-world problems? The process of agreeing on the goal increases the likelihood of choosing the best solutions and implementing them with fidelity.

Identifying Systemic and Interdependent Factors

The first element of Standard 3 challenges you to correctly identify the multiple factors that are impacting the performance of the school.

3.1 Focus on the systemic and interdependent factors in the school context that impact students' learning, school improvement, and transformation efforts.

As you worked to help others create meaning from findings, research, and inquiry, you may have guided them through preliminary performance analysis using the *Performance Factors Analysis Worksheet* (Tool 2.1) introduced in the previous chapter. This tool helped those you were facilitating to reflect on the factors in the work, workers, and workplace that they believed were impacting student performance. You may have also engaged them in reaching shared agreements about gaps in improvement and their priorities using the *Performance Gap and Priority Matrix* (Tool 2.8). If not, now is the time to use those tools. If you have used those tools with your group, review the outputs of those exercises to

- identify and record the gaps that must be closed and in what order.
- analyze the selected gaps to ensure that all significant barriers to performance have been identified.
- analyze the selected gaps to identify opportunities to raise the performance targets to exceed standards and to prepare students, teachers, and school leaders for the 21st century.
- prepare a summary containing findings and recommendations and a supporting presentation of your performance analysis and preview of the next steps for the sponsor of your efforts and the groups you are guiding.

Getting people to focus on what is happening and why the current state is what it is what it is requires lifting the stigma of admitting that everything is not working as well as it could. You will guide the group to look at factors contributing to the current state at three levels:

1. In the **work**—Identify what is being done by students, teachers, teacher leaders, administrators, and school leaders.

2. In the **workers** or people—Identify the capabilities and motives of the students, teachers, teacher leaders, administrators, and school leaders.

3. In the **workplace**—Identify the environments and surroundings in which the people live, study, and work.

It is helpful to remind the group that most factors that impact performance are not rooted in the people but within the work (how it is designed and supported) and within the workplace (the adequacy and appropriateness of the physical and emotional space) in which learning and teaching happen. When you guide the group to look at behaviors, it is often helpful to remind them that *behavior*—what people do—is a product of various factors, of which only a few are under the control of the people who do the work. For example, if teachers in various subject areas are told that they are expected to collaborate with peers to develop standards-based lessons across the curriculum to improve students' reading comprehension and problem-solving skills, they must have time in the school day to work together. They are not likely to be in control of the school schedule, which dictates times when teachers can work together. Administrators usually set the schedule. If teachers are expected to deliver the results (effective lessons) through their behaviors (collaborative planning and teaching), then they must have the factor of time that is managed by others. A performance factor that is deemed as rooted in the *workers* must be entirely within the control of those workers—in this example, a group of teachers.

Extending our example, "*If* teachers are to collaboratively develop lessons across the curriculum to improve reading comprehension and problem-solving skills while teaching the content in each subject, *then* the following are required for them to deliver those results effectively: the time and a place to collaborate."

There are a number of approaches you might use to facilitate the group in its analysis of the work, workplace, and the workers to better understand the current situation. This field guide describes three approaches; however, there are a number of references to other approaches in the resource section at the end of this book.

The *Systemic Performance Factors Review Worksheet* (Tool 3.1) is useful for leading others in a systemic review of performance factors. It begins by looking at the current state. It has questions that lead to discussion about the causes and factors that are contributing to the current state and includes questions that are meant to facilitate discussions about what interventions are needed to produce the desired state.

You can also use this tool to guide the sponsor of your efforts through *performance analysis*, asking questions that collect information about the work, workers, and workplace to help the sponsor personally identify the systemic factors that impact performance. Once you have collected this input, explain that you have already or plan to collect information from other sources that will corroborate their view and ensure that the problem is solved as quickly as possible and that the results are sustainable. You may offer a short example of how you saved time and money in the past through performance analysis, taking the time to look systemically at the factors impacting performance and results so that the right problems were solved and the results were sustained.

After you have collected and analyzed the current state of performance and have learned what others think needs to be improved and why, organize your findings so you can present them to the sponsor and any others whose support you will need. Sharing what you have learned provides facts, even if some of the facts are perception information such as teacher engagement survey data, and helps make the case for digging deeper into the causes before attempting solutions.

Occasionally at this point, you may hear people saying, "Why are we spending all this time analyzing? Why don't we just go ahead and fix what needs to be fixed?"

To move past resistance in the performance analysis phase and to have the time and resources needed to identify systemic causes, the following steps are required:

trying to name the num

Name the num

1. Ask those you are facilitating to share what they think is needed and why.

2. Assure them you will help them customize and tailor a set of solutions that best fit their situation.

3. Have the group articulate why they want to focus on this improvement at this time and what data or information has brought them to the point of expecting action and improvement now, before studying the causes.

4. Ask them to define the results they want achieved.

5. Ask them what evidence they can point to that shows that the people who work in the schools are ready to make all the required changes and all the right support is in place for them to change and deliver the desired results and to sustain those results.

6. Ask them what is causing people not to deliver the needed results.

Cause

Once the group has discussed the situation, you are in position to guide them through the *cause analysis*, to come to understand the true reasons for underperformance and what is preventing students, teachers, and school leaders from reaching higher levels of performance.

A simple and useful cause analysis process is commonly known as *The Five Whys.* Facilitate the group to pick one of the factors preventing the desired performance and ask why that factor is occurring and record the answer. Then ask why that answer is occurring and repeat until you have asked *why* five times for five different answers.

For example, a group identified the current state as "teaching to the test at the recall level," which was impacting instruction and preventing reaching the desired state of "students use higher-order thinking skills while mastering content standards." Their school improvement specialist asked the group

5W

1. "*Why* are we teaching at the recall level?" The group said, "Our students have to meet the standards on annual high-stakes tests."

Next, the facilitator asked,

2. "*Why* is that focus on high-stakes tests a barrier?" The group replied, "Because we are spending time drilling them to prepare for the test rather than guiding them to learn the content and apply it in problem solving."

Next, the facilitator asked,

3. "*Why* are you not teaching them to master the content and use it to solve problems?" The group replied, "We are not using instructional practices that support using the content to solve problems."

Tool 3.1   Systemic Performance Factors Review Worksheet

Guidelines: Focus on one problem the group wants to analyze. Identify whose performance they want to analyze—students in a specific grade or class, teachers for a specific subject? The far left column can be used to record what is expected or should be happening. In the right column, record the behaviors that need to change to improve the situation. Next, ask questions about the people who are in a position to influence the behaviors of the group whose performance you want to improve, and identify what they must do to influence the changes. The second set of questions is about who has control and what can be done to enable the target group to adopt new behaviors that will lead to the desired outcomes. When the group finishes, ask them what insights they have gained and how they want to use what they have uncovered. You can then help the group further validate their conclusions and develop an action plan to improve the situation. The example that follows focuses on student performance. You can modify this worksheet to analyze teachers, staff, administrators, and others' performance factors. Figure 3.1 is an example.

Figure 3.1   Sample Systemic Performance Factors Review Worksheet

What results are expected of students?	→	What are the current student results?
What must students do to achieve those results?	→	What are they doing now that must change or stop?
What could others (teachers, leaders, parents) be doing to support those results?	→	What are they doing that they could change or stop?
What is inside others' control that needs to change?	→	What must be done to make that change? Who must do it?
What in their work or workplace, outside their control, prevents them from doing what is needed?	→	What must be done to address barriers they cannot control? Who must do it?

Next, the facilitator asked,

4. "*Why* are you not using those practices?" The group replied, "We have not developed lessons or projects for our students to apply content to solving problems."

Finally, the facilitator asked,

5. "*Why* have you not developed those lessons or projects?" The group answered, "We don't have time to develop them, and we need training and coaching in how to deliver that type of guided learning so we continue to teach students to recall content."

Using *The Five Whys* questions in Tool 3.2, the facilitator helped the group identify the true causes of underperformance: perceived lack of time and lack of capacity-building, both causes that were under the control of the organization and administrators.

Another approach uses an adaptation of an *Ishikawa* or *fishbone* diagram for taking all the information you have collected and digging deeper. The *Adapted Fishbone* (Tool 3.3) is especially useful for helping groups see the relationships between what is and what they want and the contributing factors.

After performance analysis and cause analysis, you can determine if you are ready to move ahead to intervention selection. Facilitate the group to answer the following questions:

1. Do we have sufficient understanding of the performance gap, and are we confident in our understanding?

2. Do we have hypotheses of the causes of the performance gap?

Tool 3.2   The Five Whys

Guidelines: To use the five whys, start with a discrete problem, and then draft five questions. The exact questions you will use will depend on the answers you get to the previous question. Your goal is to surface the rationale, beliefs, and logic behind the group's conclusions about why a problem exists, what is contributing to that problem, who is or is not contributing or being affected, and what is in their control. Once you have your answers, you can ask the group about what causes they can affect and what they think about what they uncovered. Use their answers to validate their beliefs and to identify possible interventions.

Tool 3.3   Adapted Fishbone

Guidelines: Place a descriptor of the current state on the circle on the left of the diagram, and the desired state on the circle on the right side. Facilitate the development of categories to be listed on the "large bones," which represent key performance factors the group has identified relative to the gap between current and desired performance. The example shown in Figure 3.2 focuses on building capacity to improve results.

Figure 3.2   Example Adapted Fishbone

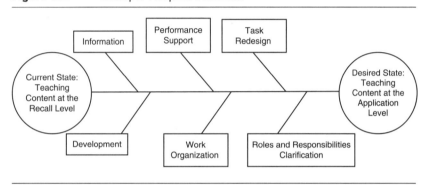

Next, you would facilitate the group in identifying the influencing factors of each one of the major categories. Figure 3.3 illustrates how a group brainstormed the causes underlying each performance factor.

Figure 3.3   Enhanced Adapted Fishbone

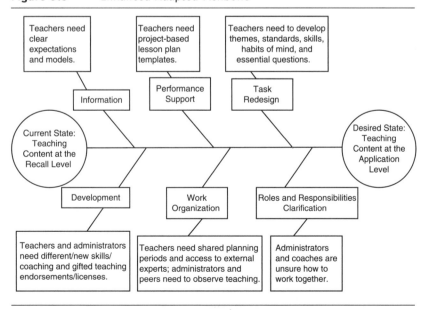

Selecting a Suite of Aligned Interventions

The second element in Standard 3 is about using the best combination of interventions to accomplish the goals of the project. Once you have answered these questions, you are in a position to continue the discussion about what needs to be done to improve the performances of students, teachers, teacher leaders, administrators, and school leaders. The second element of Standard 3 is about selecting the best combination of actions to improve the performance of the people you are focusing on, whether that be students, teachers, or school leaders.

> 3.2 Demonstrate use and alignment of a portfolio of improvement options and approaches.

Research by S. Wile and Erica Gilmore indicates that "Causes come in 3's, while solutions come in 4's," meaning that for every problem, there are usually at least three contributing factors or root causes and that at least four possible solutions are required to fix the problem (Gilmore, 2008; Wile, 1996). The fourth solution is almost always about building capability or providing performance support. For example, a group may identify a gap in student performance in mathematics. There could be a number of causes, including lack of time to study because students are overly engaged in extracurricular activities or have to work after school, ineffective instructional methods, or student peer pressure to not be "seen as a brain." No single intervention will fix the problem. Instead, what is required is a combination of coaching teachers and students; counseling students and parents in how to set more realistic goals; coaching students' study habits; and creating performance aids. The point is that one solution is rarely sufficient to achieve and sustain the results you want.

Your role is to facilitate the selection of a combination of solutions that collectively are best suited to the needs of the school identified during the analysis phase and will make the best use of the available resources. Interventions or solutions can be classified in many different ways; this field guide classifies them by whether they are intended to improve the workers, work, or the workplace.

 *Interventions for Improving Workers' Performance*

Interventions focused on **building people's capability** include the following:

\ *Providing Developmental Opportunities*—Offer training, provide coaching and mentoring, or establish developmental assignments (i.e., project-based, in-class, and self-study) so that people can develop the skills and knowledge required to carry out the tasks expected of them.

2 *Providing Performance Support*—Develop or secure protocols, job aids, tools, equipment, instructional guides, and so on so that people have access to the cognitive and physical supports required to build proficiency and can carry out their tasks repeatedly to standard.

3 *Reframing*—Offer a different perspective on the situation so people see new possibilities and do not remain stuck in the old paradigms of what was and what can be. Examples include funding, providing release time so people can participate in instruction on how to do the work before them, and providing access to support tools and protocols (i.e., job aids, rubrics, books, and laptops) to help them build proficiency.

Interventions for Improving the Work

These capacity-building interventions will be less effective if they not supported by other types of changes that **improve the work**:

Setting and Clarifying Expectations—Be explicit about what people are expected to accomplish in their job or role. Do not assume that the job description adequately describes the expected deliverables or outputs.

Giving Feedback—Give people constructive comments about what they have or have not accomplished and how they are executing their assignments; design tasks so they include the standards of performance and the measures of success, so people can judge the adequacy of their work. This goes beyond the annual performance review and creates expectations for changes in practice based on feedback that is specific and based on review of targeted behaviors, outcomes, and results.

Providing Information—Codify and document the information people require to do their jobs and make it accessible; ensure that people have the information they need, including goals, performance metrics, task information, and feedback so that people know what is expected of them, have access to the information they need to do the task, and know how well they are doing.

Designing the Job or Task—Structure the work. This includes the activities, processes, procedures, and interfaces required to support students' learning, teachers' instruction, administration, and leadership so that work can be done efficiently and effectively.

Clarifying Roles and Responsibilities—Clarify job descriptions, task assignments, reporting relationships, team assignments, and the like to eliminate confusion, make optimal use of resources, and enable development of new skills and relationships.

Providing Consequences—Recognize, reward, or impose consequences on actions that influence the behaviors of students, teachers, leader teachers, administrators, and school leaders so that constructive behaviors are reinforced and destructive ones are extinguished.

Providing Resources—Secure, replace, and upgrade the resources (including time, equipment, space, and access to others) that people need to do the work so that they can effectively accomplish their performance objectives.

Interventions for Improving the Workplace

Interventions that improve the work must be supported by capacity-building interventions and interventions that improve the **workplace environment**:

Creating a Supportive Culture—In order to create a supportive culture, multiple workplace factors must be considered:

○ Examine and address the messages, behaviors, and priorities of all of the people involved in terms of how they do or do not support the school improvement goals.

○ Analyze and address the physical layout and condition of the buildings and grounds to ensure that they are safe, clean, and support the activities of the school.

○ Evaluate and address the capability of the infrastructure, so it supports the use of new technologies (electronic white boards, laptops, digital tools).

○ Establish norms and rituals for the teachers, administrators, and leaders, so they model respect, collaboration, and a focus on meaningful results.

Providing Leadership Direction—Execute the leadership behaviors that provide the guidance people require, including acting as a spokesperson, representing the opinions of students and teachers to external stakeholders, negotiating for resources, and mediating disputes. You must ensure that leaders consistently communicate a strategic direction, build alliances, provide leadership coaching, and serve as role models so students, teachers, and administrators can stay focused on what is important and act with confidence.

Doing Workforce Planning and Talent Management—Identify the capabilities required for today's work and the work of the future and assess the capabilities of the current workforce to identify deficiencies and gaps. This allows the organization to develop strategies to attract, retain, and develop people with the required capabilities for today and tomorrow's work.

Building Strategic Alliances—Establish relationships with community agencies, service providers, and business leaders to ensure that the school has access to resources that support learning and the development of 21st-century skills.

Measuring—Capture and analyze data that measure what people do, what is accomplished, what has changed, and so on. Set baselines so growth can be measured and interventions can be revised in a timely manner.

Ensuring Governance and Oversight—Establish accountability for providing direction, advocating for resources, defining goals, setting expectations, mediating disputes, and authorizing the use of resources. If those involved perceive that someone is in charge and is setting the appropriate direction for the school, their confidence in their ability to reach their goals is likely to increase.

Aligning—Revisit how resources are allocated and what behaviors are reinforced so that they are aligned with the school's vision, mission, goals, action plans, and performance metrics.

Many potential interventions exist to improve workers' capacity, the work, and the workplace environment. Your role is to help those you are guiding to select the most appropriate set of solutions to collectively address the causes of underperformance and that support transformation.

Facilitate the group in the process of brainstorming possibilities for solutions based on their analysis of the situation. The *Intervention Selection Guide* (Tool 3.4) can help you guide your group in selecting solutions designed to address the factors causing poor or underperformance in the schools you're working with.

Tool 3.4   Intervention Selection Guide

Guidelines: Ask the group to list the underlying causes contributing to underperformance. Next, ask a series of questions to help the group identify the interventions they think will have the highest probability of addressing the underlying causes. Have the group look critically at their recommended solutions to ensure that they address the actual cause and are comprehensive enough to bring about and sustain the desired change.

1. If the cause is _____, what can we do to eliminate or mitigate the cause?

2. Whose behavior has to change?

3. What four things might we do to support this change to solve the problem and improve performance?

4. Whose support do we need?

5. What could we do to develop people's capability to do the new work?

   a. Developmental opportunities

   b. Performance support

   c. Reframing

6. What could we do to improve the work that is required?

   a. Clarify expectations

   b. Provide feedback

   c. Provide information

   d. Redesign the work

   e. Clarify roles and responsibilities

   f. Provide consequences

   g. Provide new or different resources

7. What could we do to improve the workplace environment?

   a. Change the culture

   b. Improve leadership

   c. Implement a talent/workforce management process

   d. Develop strategic alliances

   e. Provide governance

   f. Measure performance

   g. Confirm that our practices are aligned with our vision, mission, and goals

Building Higher-Order Skills

The third element under Standard 3 has to do with building higher-order skills.

> 3.3 Ensure improvement and transformation efforts result in school teams and students demonstrating higher-order thinking skills, collaboration, effective use of technology, and other skills that create value.

As the facilitator of school improvement, you will be expected to get the adults you are guiding to do the same things students need to do: communicate, collaborate, think critically, and create. Penny Smith, a highly effective Certified School Improvement Specialist, has been a leader in maintaining high expectations and increasing student achievement for diverse populations of students as a principal and as a performance consultant. She points to the focus on systemic performance factors as an opportunity to change the thinking and behavior of adult problem solvers:

> Application of skills and problem-based learning is a critical component to twenty-first century learning. There are many ways to solve problems, so encourage divergent thinking as opposed to . . . [discouraging] it. By considering multiple strategies for solving problems, students learn to validate their learning and display efficacy as they develop skills that transfer across content areas. By facilitating adults to think and act as twenty-first century learners they can not only solve problems to support student success, but also address the factors that impact their job satisfaction, performance and results, and learning and growth. (P. Smith, personal communication, September, 10, 2011)

As you facilitate the improvement process, be explicit that the critical thinking inquiry, collaborative learning, and problem solving the adults in the school are engaging in is the type of work and skills teachers must teach their students to perform and master to make them successful in the future. When students or the adults that work in the school use project-based learning, they model and master the type of collaboration and higher-order thinking skills that can solve real-world problems. Your role at this time in the process is to help the adults in the school work together and use problem-solving tools and skills to define and agree upon the gaps in performance, why the gaps exist, and the suite of aligned systemic solutions that will solve problems and achieve breakthroughs in performance.

AN EXAMPLE OF AN EFFECTIVE APPLICATION OF STANDARD 3

Elise Robreaux had deep expertise in curriculum, assessment, and instruction and worked as an associate superintendent assigned to guide school administrators and their faculty and staff to improve student achievement. She identified a group of overage students in the 9th and 10th grades in the three high schools within the school district who were causing discipline problems and whose academic performance was well below that of their peers. She knew that research shows that these students are at high risk to drop out of school. She reviewed the school improvement plans from each of the high schools and brought together the principals, a counselor, and a teacher from each school as well as an external stakeholder from each school's leadership team.

First, Robreaux engaged the group in performance analysis, analyzing the students' test scores and samples of their work from classroom assignments in English/language arts, math, social studies, and science. Additionally, the team looked at attendance and discipline data and their academic performance history for every year these students had been in the school system. After the analysis, she facilitated the group to state what they found as a problem statement that reflected the performance gap:

> We have identified a group of overage, underperforming students in Grades 9 and 10 who are not on track academically with their peers and who need interventions that will accelerate their learning.

Next, she guided them to state what the goal is and agree on it:

> Our goal is to get 100 percent of these students back on track within 18 months and reduce the likelihood that they will drop out in the future.

Next, she facilitated the group in describing the gap from the data and information they reviewed. The group described what they had discovered through their initial inquiry:

> (1) Almost all of these students were struggling with reading, writing, and numeracy; (2) their academic histories, where available, showed that they had fallen behind several years before and had not caught up; (3) of the students who had been in their school last year, most had been absent more than ten days in the last year; (4) three of the students were homeless and twelve were working to support their families; and (5) these students were accounting for 80 percent of the discipline referrals in the school.

When teachers were interviewed and asked to predict if these students could get back on track and graduate within two years, they indicated low levels of confidence in the idea that the students would graduate.

Robreaux guided the group to analyze and define the performance factors in the work, workers, and workplace that were preventing this group of students from getting back on track and becoming ready to graduate. The group identified the following:

Work factors: Interim assessments reveal that the students are not making the same level of progress as their peers, but instruction continues at the same rate for every student. Teachers are providing the students with learning assignments aligned to the annual high-stakes assessments, but teachers have not engaged in diagnosis of student performance to identify the trends in the students' work that would reveal the parts of the curriculum that they have not mastered to create readiness for the work at their current grade level. When students miss work assignments, they routinely are awarded 0s, with no opportunity to complete the missing assignments. No resources have been provided to help these students repair or recover credits and to progress. Since these students are being treated the same as all other students, they appear to be individual exceptions to achievement, rather than a group with similar characteristics and needs. Teachers have not been provided time to work together to analyze longitudinal student performance.

Worker factors: Teachers do not expect the students to meet standards, and not all teachers have been trained or coached in differentiation of instruction and other teaching practices that could help the students catch up with their peers. Teachers are overwhelmed by trying to help all their students do well on their tests.

Workplace factors: These students' schedules are the same as students who are on track, with no time for extra scheduled support. Many of these students are either absent or suspended, reducing their learning time. Their teachers have not had training in teaching reading within the high school curriculum or differentiation of instruction. Classroom observations reveal limited differentiation of instruction to meet these students where they are and take them to the levels where they could be performing.

After guiding the teachers to define the factors impacting the gap in students' performance, the team broke into smaller groups and analyzed the causes behind the performance factors they had identified in the work, workplace, and workers using *The Five Whys* and the *Adapted Fishbone*. The group compiled a list of systemic causes their analysis produced. Next, Robreaux helped them sort the brainstormed and researched causes into categories using the *Intervention Selection Guide*.

The group pointed to the following types of interventions to address the causes:

Information:

- Study and communicate historical performance data.
- Collect data to identify the students who made up the group who were both overage and underperforming.
- Identify teachers with demonstrated capability to differentiate instruction to meet students' needs.

Consequences:

- Provide positive attention for teachers who were using instructional methods and operating from beliefs that benefited these students who were off track.
- Assign two teachers who indicate interest, belief, and ability to accelerate the students in a special pull-out program for the group of students.
- Provide opportunities for students in the pull-out group to participate in special activities, such as sporting events, pizza during study time, and earned flexibility in their schedules.

Design/Redesign:

- Reorganize the schedule of the students and teachers to allow teachers to have common planning times and to coordinate instruction between the pull-out teachers and other teachers working with the students.
- Provide access to online courses and credit-recovery programs that allow students to earn credits needed to get back on track and to master the curriculum that will be needed to complete school within two years.
- Extend the school day and evening and weekend instruction in the areas the students need to master to catch up.
- Provide rigorous academic work to accelerate their learning and performance, rather than focusing only on remediation.
- Differentiate instruction in regular classrooms aligned to the instruction in their pull-out group.
- Use interviewing and hiring protocols to select and assign teachers who have the skills to differentiate instruction.
- Use flexible grouping and other strategies that impact student achievement.

Capacity and Capability Building:

- Select two teachers with the capacity and capability to design and deliver the instruction the students need and to apply the tools and resources provided to help the students catch up with their peers.
- Use common planning time to provide training on identification of overage and underperforming students and their gaps in achievement.
- Train teachers to differentiate instruction and use peer observation of teachers who have demonstrated capability.
- Assign academic coaches to work with teachers to change and improve their instructional practices to meet student needs.

Alignment:

- Ensure that the school improvement plan includes goals, strategies, and performance targets for overage and underperforming students.
- Align expectations for teachers with performance appraisals.
- Align assessments to the curriculum.
- Align professional learning for teachers and administrators to student performance needs.
- Assign teachers with the skills needed to support the group of overage students to develop and implement an improvement plan with targets aligned with the school improvement plan and school performance targets.
- Align resources (time, talent, tools, resources, and funding) to support the selected interventions.

Leadership/Supervision:

- Establish a vision for the success of all students, including the overage and underperforming students.
- Help teachers reframe thinking about the potential for these students to succeed.
- Provide clear expectations.
- Monitor, measure, and coach performance against clear performance criteria.
- Allocate resources and provide support needed for teachers to help students meet their performance targets.

- Determine the performance interventions and process improvements that are needed day-to-day to support teaching and learning for this group of students.
- Work with stakeholders to develop additional support for the students and to increase student engagement.

Governance:

- Ensure that policies and budgets support the type of changes and interventions needed to support the group of overage and underperforming students.
- Advocate for community leaders, external partners, and financial aid to support interventions that address the needs of the group of overage and underperforming students.
- Adjust policies to prevent students from missing needed instructional time.

Using the list of interventions that the group had generated, the group worked through the list and sorted the interventions to indicate those that could produce the needed results most efficiently. The group selected the following suite of solutions:

1. Form a pull-out group of the identified overage students.

2. Organize time in the school day for the students to work with two teachers who have the interest, capability, and disposition to engage and accelerate the students.

3. Allocate resources to these interventions (time, funding, space, tools, equipment, etc.).

4. Develop an acceleration curriculum for the students, aligned with their curriculum in their regular classes.

5. Provide support to the pull-out teachers and develop the capacity of all teachers to differentiate instruction and use flexible grouping and other instructional practices that can help keep students from falling behind their peers.

6. Change policies to create extra instructional time for students who are impacted by external forces (homelessness, lack of family support, need to work, child care needs, etc.) that impact learning time.

7. Use technology to accelerate credit recovery and reduce gaps in knowledge.

8. Provide motivation and support for the students, including pizza during extended learning sessions and social and emotional support from mentors.

9. Monitor each student's response to the interventions and adapt as necessary.

10. Celebrate the students' and teachers' progress and results.

Robreaux addressed the group:

We have identified some promising interventions. You should be very proud of the work you are designing for both teachers and these students. We are almost ready to develop and record a plan to guide the work ahead. I want to ask you one more question: Will the interventions we have selected ensure that this group of students will not only catch up to meet standards but will also develop the skills needed to succeed in postsecondary learning and the world of work?

After further discussion, the group brainstormed two more interventions:

1. Engage each student in an assignment that connects that student with someone in the community who had been both academically successful and successful in his or her career. Guide the students to interview the adults and work in groups to compile the characteristics of successful adults and make electronic presentations of their success factors, supported by at least two research sources for each characteristic.

2. Engage the students in learning expeditions in which they identify and develop a solution for reducing waste in the school and community while meeting a set of content standards and performance task standards provided by their pull-out teachers and regular teachers in a jointly designed assignment.

Robreaux acknowledged the hard work of the group and gave them a preview of the work ahead to plan and document the work as a systemic improvement project.

AN EXAMPLE OF A LESS EFFECTIVE APPLICATION OF STANDARD 3

Sal Camp was assigned to work with a school district with average performance to support the district in transformation efforts that would increase student learning and better prepare students for college and careers. When Sal arranged the first meeting with the superintendent of the district, he had already collected a great deal of data related to the performance of the schools in the district. During this first interview with the superintendent in the school district, he learned that the district had recently been awarded a grant to support giving every student in Grades 4–12 a tablet PC to support his or her learning. When Sal asked the superintendents about the performance and outcomes targeted by the implementation of the One-to-One (one electronic device per student) Initiative, he was told that several other school districts were making the same change and that the superintendent thought it would be good for students and would reduce the costs associated with textbooks.

When Sal explained that he was going to conduct a performance analysis to ensure that all the improvement needs and barriers to student success were addressed, the superintendent replied, "When I brought you in to help us, I was thinking you would lead the implementation of the One-to-One initiative. We already know our data and have school improvement plans in every school. I just want to get this grant awarded, so we can give the electronic tools to the students. We don't need to spend time and money on analyzing what already exists. We need to move ahead on this technology adoption. Please review the grant we developed to get the funding and tell me what we need to do to make this happen."

Sal reviewed the grant and each school's improvement plan and concluded that the implementation of the initiative was not aligned to the existing improvement plans. After interviewing the district's technology director, he realized that the work that would need to be done to support successful adoption of the new tools was not yet identified. He could see that there were multiple factors that would impact the outcome of the project but felt certain that the superintendent was not focused on those potential barriers. He decided to do what the superintendent had asked, but he worried that the systemic changes needed to support the initiative were not recognized and that the adoption of the tools was not aligned with intentional efforts to improve teaching, learning, and student achievement or to develop the critical skills students would need in the future.

REFLECTION

Compare and contrast the approaches that Robreaux and Camp used in facilitating change.

1. What did Robreaux do that made a positive difference?

2. In your opinion, what prevented Camp from making more progress with the school team?

3. What in this chapter will be useful to you in your practice of facilitating improvement?

POWER POINTS

As you continue to develop your skills in facilitating school improvement, consider the following:

- Avoid embracing a single solution at the exclusion of others.
- If the group is determined to focus on one answer, reframe that solution as a vehicle that will transport other interventions as it is implemented. For example, if the group believes that adopting an electronic system that contains lesson plans will improve students' math skills, support its use and then ask the group to do the following:
  - Come up with a plan to support teachers in learning how to use the new software.
  - Identify when in the school day students might practice lessons using the new tool.
  - Identify ways for students to work together on the use of the new software; compare lesson in the software with lessons used on class.
  - Recognize teachers and students who do collaborate and then document and share what they learned from having used the new software.
  - Suggest ways to monitor students' math progress.
  - Document and publicly post all of the things the group has identified it wants to implement to support student learning, teacher performance, higher level skills, and so on.
  - Communicate the group's commitment to solving the problem.

SUMMARY

This chapter in some ways is the heart of the book, because it addresses the need for a more holistic approach to school improvement. It recognizes that the job of improving schools is very complex just as the schools are complex social political entities. As a school improvement specialist, you have to guide the group in uncovering what is real and what is surmised. You will help them critically examine the schools system's commitment to building capability, how the work is laid out, and the degree to which the workplace environment supports learning today's skills and those needed for the 21st century. There is a natural tendency to grab on to obvious solutions; however, if the group does not address the requirements of the people, how their work is defined and designed, and the capacity of the workplace environment to reinforce and sustain the new behaviors, the odds of their interventions being effective are low. At the same time, this chapter points to the need to be both near- and farsighted. You have to work with the group given where they are, what they are ready to accept, and what they have the energy to embrace while getting them to lay the ground work for the future. Schools cannot build 21st-century skills if children cannot master the basic skills. However, there is an opportunity to revisit the effectiveness of today's instructional practices, how work is allocated, and what behaviors are best to reinforce.

See the end of the book for a complete list of resources and references related to identifying systemic factors.

Additional materials and resources related to
The School Improvement Specialist Field Guide
can be found on the companion website.
http://www.corwin.com/sisguide

Plan and Record 4

[handwritten: Aassword — webote]

Real World Challenge
Bailey's Story, Part 4

Frank Perez could hear the excitement in Bailey Pittman's voice when she called to report her progress. "We have been able to identify the underlying causes that are holding this school back," she said. "We divided our focus into three categories: First, we focused on the workers *(what adults in the school do or don't do that impacts what students are willing and able to do). Next, we focused on the* work- place *(what in the school context helps or prevents adults from doing what they could for students) and the* work *(what processes are needed or are not working as they could). I worked with the principal, the school leadership team, and teams of teachers and staff to discuss potential solutions and agree on the changes that are needed. They have identified a comprehensive set of operational, instructional, cultural, developmental, and support interventions. I can feel the resistance slipping away. People are beginning to agree that they can transform this school and how they can do it. There is a lot of work ahead."*

[handwritten: RMS]

"Congratulations," Frank replied. "Isn't it rewarding when people can begin to see possibilities and commit to make the needed changes happen? It sounds like you have a great deal of positive momentum that can be leveraged to get people working together on the interventions. Have you thought about how you are going to help them plan and structure those improvement projects so they carry them out successfully?"

"I have helped them add each of the initiatives to the school improvement plan so that we keep all the efforts aligned," Bailey replied. "The principal and I have identified the key people who will be engaged in each of the initiatives, and we are working with them to think through what needs to be done. I am doing a great deal of coaching right now, helping them decide exactly what they will do and how."

*[handwritten: Next steps *]*

"Sounds like you have a good start," Frank observed. "From my experience, this is the time to get everyone in the habit of writing down and communicating what they are going to do, when they are going to do it, and what progress and success will look like. Thinking through and writing down simple work plans or project plans can help people know what is expected, support the monitoring of all the various efforts underway, and keep everyone focused on the work they have committed to do. I know that the idea of taking the time to commit their chosen initiatives to writing and develop work plans might be foreign at first, but the effort pays huge dividends. It is also the same type of planning teachers will guide students to do in project-based learning in their classrooms. Teaching them to plan their projects so

87

*their progress and results can be assessed is good professional learning for support-
ing teaching that builds higher-order thinking skills."*

"Are those work plans part of the school improvement plan?" Bailey asked.

*"You might think of them as a roadmap for how the school's improvement plan
is implemented through the interventions they have identified. I think of them as
part of the planning process but also as the underpinnings of the management and
accountability processes for implementing improvement projects. Also, if work
plans are written and you or any of the other individuals involved in leading implementation of the interventions are hit by a bus, the rest of the team knows what
has to be done and keeps the work moving forward," he advised. "Of course, I am
joking about the bus part, but it does pay to make sure everyone knows what to do
and can pick up the work when a team member is away."*

*"I will do my best to avoid being hit by a bus," Bailey laughed, "but I see what
you mean. Does this have to be complicated? I am afraid if I ask people to do too
much planning, they will lose their enthusiasm for the work ahead."*

*"You only need to plan the work that you want people to do well," Frank
teased. "Keep your work plans simple: what, who, by when, resources, milestones to check progress and expected evidence. As they say, 'Plan the work
and work the plan.' Best of all, when an improvement project is completed, there is
a roadmap for replicating it when needed."*

To be continued . . .

STANDARD 4: PLAN AND RECORD

Standard 4 focuses on planning and recording the improvements to be
made. In earlier chapters, you focused on the dual nature of the role of a
school improvement specialist as both *expert* and *facilitator*. The depth of
your expertise will allow you to effectively coach those you are guiding
through each of the interventions they have agreed to implement to bring
about the needed improvements. Coaching them through each step and
guiding their work can and will lead to the desired improvements; however, if you have not helped them learn to plan their work and how they
will assess it along the way, you have failed to help them develop the key
skills and discipline they need for long-term success when you are no longer
there to coach them. You are not only there to teach them improved practices and help them implement them. You are there to help them learn and
institutionalize a process for continuous improvement and transformation.

You are responsible for making sure the right work is planned and
supported for students *and* for adults. This will require you to guide those
who lead the organization in recognizing that they are accountable for
managing the performance factors in the work and the workplace that
impact adult performance and, by extension, student performance. You
might explain that as, "If students are going to succeed at x, then the

organization must plan how to best support adults to succeed at y, where x equals all the outcomes and targeted results for students and y equals all the outcomes and targeted results of the adults."

> If students are going to succeed at x, then the organization must plan how to best support adults to succeed at y, where x equals all the outcomes and targeted results for students and y equals all the outcomes and targeted results of the adults.

Recommending What Works

The first element in Standard 4 is about leveraging what others have found that works.

4.1 Recommend methods, resources, and high-impact practices and information about what works to address the factors impacting performance.

After the improvement initiatives have been selected and those you are guiding are ready to begin their work, your expertise will allow you to help them to think through how they are going to do the work. One way to do this is to frame the improvement project with a guiding question, just as you would as a teacher guiding project-based learning. For example, if the group you are working with is focused on an initiative to reduce interruptions to individual student and classroom learning time and increase collaborative learning time, coach them to frame it as a driving question or challenge, such as "How can we reduce interruptions and increase collaborative learning time across the curriculum?" Ask them to give a name to the project. In this case, they might call it something like *Time Together*. List the project on a *Project Commitment Agreement* form shown in Tool 4.1.

Note that the approval of the commitment agreement ensures that the appropriate sponsor of the project will support it and is aware of what is to be planned and carried out in the school. This ensures the needed support and alignment.

Next, by acting as the expert, you can teach those you are guiding what you know about the topic and direct them to resources to find the research-based best practices for answering the question and formulating the improvement project. By acting as the facilitator, guide them to study together and select the practices they want them to use; keep a running list of the *how*s for solving the problem. This list of *how*s is the beginning of documentation of their work plan or project plan. As they record each *how*, coach them to be explicit and communicate to others what they are doing and what they intend to accomplish. This coaching is critical to embedding a process for improvement in the school that will continue

Tool 4.1   Project Commitment Agreement

Guidelines: This form is intended to help you communicate the importance of the group's commitment to the work. Begin by asking the group a driving question, note how the question fits or support the school's improvement plan, and then document the group's agreement to work on that question.

Project name: _____ Date: _____

Driving question: _____

Aligned to: _____
(Goal(s) of school improvement plan and/or strategic plan)

The undersigned are committed to learn and work together to answer this question and implement a collaborative improvement project by _____ (deadline) that will produce the following evidence of success:

1. _____

2. _____

3. _____

Name: _____ Signature: _____ Date: _____

Name: _____ Signature: _____ Date: _____

Name: _____ Signature: _____ Date: _____

Approved by: _____ Date: _____

when you are not available to guide them and to create the autonomy they need to fully engage in the work, persist when the work is challenging, and take ownership of the work and results.

Developing the Plan

The next element of Standard 4 is about developing and recording the plans for the work ahead.

4.2 Facilitate development and recording of sound improvement and transformation plans with related action or project plans and progress measures.

Including the projected initiatives in the school improvement plan ensures the alignment of the efforts with the other work of the school; however, you must ensure that the *hows* that have been identified for the work ahead are recorded on a work plan. That plan must make clear who will do what work, who will supervise it and support it, who is accountable, the outcomes and results they are accountable for, when certain milestones should be reached and when the project should be completed, the support and resources that will be applied, and how and when progress will be assessed. The plan need not be complicated, but it should guide those who will do the work to think through what they will do, projecting backwards from the date they will complete the work and the results they will achieve. Guide them to complete an *Improvement Project Work Plan* (Tool 4.2) for each of the major *hows* of their project.

You can anticipate that people may at first push back on the idea of writing down their work plans, since it takes time away from the *doing* of the work. Stress that these planning skills are the same skills teachers need to transition to less teaching and more learning in their classrooms, with students engaged in projects in which they apply their new knowledge to real-world problems. Help them frame the planning process as good professional practice for developing schools, where the form and function of learning are recreated to support mastery of the types of skills students need to be successful in the work of work. Collaborative project planning is one of those skills.

Once the work plans are developed, take time to guide them through a quick check to make sure the work is going to be sustainable and can be implemented as planned. Use the *Feasibility Worksheet* in Tool 4.3 to determine if all systems are set up for project success.

If any of the feasibility factors are missing, work with the group and the sponsor of their project to determine how to satisfy those requirements or to adjust the project to account for them, so they do not derail the project or cause it to be abandoned before it can achieve the desired results.

Communicating the Work Ahead

The third element of Standard 4 focuses on communicating about the project and making performance expectations clear, both for those who do the work and those who must support it. The behaviors in this element help everyone understand why their efforts matter, how the project fits into the big picture of the school, and how their efforts are aligned to support the overall success of the school and its students.

Tool 4.2   Improvement Project Work Plan

Guidelines: Use this tool or create your own to capture what is to be done, who is doing it, when it should be done by, and what the expected outcomes or deliverables are.

Improvement Project Work Plan

Name of Project:			Duration:
Team Members:			Sponsor:
			School Improvement Plan (SIP) Goal:
Other Stakeholders Involved:			
Driving Question:			
Evidence of Success:			
How?	*What We Will Do to Make That Happen?*	*By When?*	*Who Will Do It?*

Kickoff

Communication Plan

How will we launch this project?	How will we keep people informed?

Assessments	How Will We Assess Progress During This Project? (Formative)	Milestones/When We Will Check In and Report	How We Will Measure Our Progress	Evidence We Will Collect
	How Will We Measure Results at the End of the Project and Prove Our Effectiveness? (Summative)	Performance Measures/Targets	How We Will Collect Performance Data	Final Evidence of Our Success
Resources Needed	On-site people, facilities, time:			
	Equipment, materials:			
	Support/funding:			
	Other:			
Reflection Methods	Individual	Group	Larger Group	Whole School

Tool 4.3   Feasibility Worksheet

Guidelines: Before beginning a detailed plan for the proposed initiative(s), work with the team to carefully consider the following factors, as they will predict the likelihood that the desired outcomes and results can be achieved. Any question that cannot be answered "yes" will require the team to plan how to correct or mitigate the impact of that factor. Ask the group to add any other unique local factors that could impact the viability of this improvement. Begin by asking the team to read over the questions, add those they think will help, answer the questions, and finally, reflect on how their answers will affect how they will build the project charter and action plans.

Questions	Yes/No
Does the culture of the school support the expected behaviors the project supports?	
Is sponsorship for the project and its related initiatives assured in the long term?	
Is there oversight or governance of the planned project in place beyond the immediate launch or refocus?	
Is there evidence that you can get adequate funding over the time required for the project to be effective? (For example, if a grant is available to start the work, what funding source will keep the work going after the grant expires?)	
Are expected new behaviors integrated in jobs, performance measures, and evaluations? (For example, if the new behaviors are seen as "outside of the regular work," it will be difficult to sustain them.)	
Are resources committed in the long term to support the adoption of new behaviors? (For example, will resources for retraining or coaching be available after the start-up?)	
Is the infrastructure in place to support the interventions? (Does the plan show the people, time, working arrangements, etc. needed to get the proposed work done?)	
Do current leadership and administrative practices support the new behaviors necessary to carry out the project? (For example, do job descriptions and roles and responsibilities support doing the work of the project?)	
Is there a planned process for monitoring outcomes and impact and measuring progress and results that will give feedback in time to make adjustments?	
Will the change each intervention produces be enough to outweigh the estimated cost and effort?	

Will the targeted results be accepted as achievement or success? (For example, is everyone in agreement on what effectiveness and success look like?)	
Are all proposed interventions aligned with each other so that they work together to achieve the desired state of performance and results? (For example, are improved recruiting processes aligned to the plans of the school to improve specific student outcomes?)	
Will there be a critical mass of internal stakeholders to support this effort? (Critical mass is 51 percent of the right people—those who have the influence to bring others along to support the effort, those who can offer resources or support, and those who could stall progress or prevent the work from being sustainable.)	
Will there be a critical mass of external stakeholders to support this effort?	
Other questions	

4.3 Facilitate communicating the work ahead and the individual and team performance expectations so that people's efforts are aligned and focused on meaningful activities that are more likely to lead to the desired outcomes in support of student learning and school improvement and transformation.

The *Feasibility Worksheet* is focused on two of the key predictors of success for the planned work you will guide: People know what is expected of them, and those expectations are integrated into their performance evaluations.

The *Checklist of Understanding* (Tool 4.4) can help you review items with those who supervise and support the work at hand to make sure the processes of the school (particularly communication) are aligned to support the project and vice versa.

Another useful tool, the *Communications Worksheet* (Tool 4.5), is intended to help your team accept the responsibility for keeping stakeholders informed and using the stakeholders' preferred communication methods, such as e-mail, phone, written notes, a shared site or blog, school newsletters, or other media. It also is intended to get teams to explicitly assign the responsibility for creating and disseminating messages and not just assume it will happen. Using this tool reminds the team that stakeholders and others have a right to know what is going on and helps the team avoid the problem of potentially overlooking someone who may be in a position to influence decisions about funding and the changes he or she is working to achieve. The worksheet also clarifies who is responsible for communicating and how to best keep others informed of what is happening.

Tool 4.4   Checklist of Understanding

Guidelines: Use this checklist to confirm that everyone shares the same understanding of the work ahead.

Does everyone who needs to know understand	Yes/No
the direction the work is headed?	
what they can do to contribute?	
the performance expectations?	
what will be done and by whom?	
how it will be done?	
why it will be done?	
the targeted outcomes, outputs, and results?	
the milestones and deadlines?	
the consequences of success and failure?	
how their efforts will be formally evaluated?	

Tool 4.5   Communications Worksheet

Guidelines: Use this worksheet to walk the group through decisions about how to best communicate the work they are doing. Complete the column with the information requested.

Who is kept informed?	How should media be used? What media should be used?	Who creates the message?	Who approves the message?	Who sends out the message?

If a launch or widespread communication of the project has been planned, coach those you are guiding to craft clear messages and to communicate them on one piece of paper or in seven or fewer concise slides. Also, since they have been down deep in the causes, details, and interdependent parts of the plan, it is time for them to give everyone who needs to know a glimpse of how all the parts of the planned project are aligned by using one graphic, metaphor, mental model, or chart to aggregate all the parts into a handful of easily understood concepts.

Documenting the Decisions

All the work plans and the communication processes the group develops help accomplish the last element of Standard 4.

> 4.4 Document the practices and progress so that best practices can be replicated with fidelity and taught and disseminated to others.

If you and the group are working from a written plan, albeit one that is dynamic and changing as the work evolves, you are producing a roadmap for future improvement both in the content of the plan and the improved practices it supports in the work of the school and in the process used to seek and achieve improvement and transformation. In your role as expert and guide, you are seeking to leave durable processes in place for those you have been guiding to use autonomously to achieve other types of improvements in the future and to sustain those you are currently supporting.

One key tool for documentation is a professional or project portfolio that is developed by the group or by individuals within the group who are leading the project. The portfolio can be used to capture the plan, work, outcomes, results, and evidence as the project unfolds and is a valuable asset in the performance evaluation of those accountable for the improvement effort. Certified School Improvement Specialists use an electronic portfolio, provided with their CSIS application, to document their work and evidence of proficiency in all ten of the CSIS Standards.

If you are not ready to apply for your CSIS certification, you or your organization can access the portfolio at http://www.accreditedportfolios .com. You can use the portfolio, which hosts and stores your data and information using cloud computing technology, for a small annual fee and increase your storage size as needed over time. You can use the portfolio for one project or multiple projects to showcase your best work and to share your work and evidence with peers, supervisors, employers, potential employers, and others who you want to review the evidence of your work proficiency and results.

Even if you don't use portfolios, be sure that those who do the work (including you) keep records from the past projects. They will not only help replicate good work, but they will also help to produce better future results without reinventing the wheel each time a new project is planned.

AN EXAMPLE OF AN EFFECTIVE APPLICATION OF STANDARD 4

Sophie Chu was assigned by Dr. Karla Rucker, the superintendent of Green Valley School District, to facilitate improvement of gaps in student achievement in the district's three elementary schools, one middle school, and one high school. After collecting and studying data and conducting a comprehensive performance analysis with the central office and school teams, Chu presented a report to the senior leadership group, consisting of Dr. Rucker, two associate superintendents, and the schools' principals. The report defined what the teams she facilitated had discovered about the district's current performance and the performance that would be needed not only to ensure that all students met standards but also to ensure that they have a good chance of succeeding in the future—both in academics and in the world of work in the remainder of the 21st century.

Chu used qualitative and quantitative data to pinpoint the performance factors that were impacting student, adult, and organizational results. Using a chart, she reported the results of the cause analysis sessions, organized by causes rooted in the work; the school, school district, and community environment; and the students and the adults impacting student performance. Finally, she presented a list of recommended interventions, aligned to all the identified performance factors and causes, along with the sources of research and other evidence that supported those interventions as potential solutions.

Following a discussion of the findings and recommendations, Dr. Rucker polled the senior leadership group regarding their willingness to move ahead with the recommendations. After expressing some concerns about whether some team members in the schools and district office would be willing and able to make all the needed changes, the group agreed that the proposed solutions were promising and needed but would be difficult. Dr. Rucker then asked Chu about how things might proceed. "It seems we agree that we have many strengths to build on, but we also have some gaps in our performance that we need to close. We see that there are some underlying causes that must be addressed to close those gaps and ensure our students master the content of their courses and gain the kinds of skills they will need to be successful in the future. What are the next steps? Do you have a plan?"

"If you are all ready to move ahead," Chu replied, "it is time to begin the work by planning process for these projects and their related initiatives. I have reviewed the existing strategic plan and the district and school improvement plans, and we have some alignment to do to ensure those plans are updated to include the improvements you are now agreeing to target."

"Also, my experience has taught me," she continued, "and research into effective change management in schools confirms that people must help to develop their own work plans if they are going to support the implementation of those plans and be accountable for the outcomes and results. They need to be engaged in planning the suites of solutions so they recognize interdependencies in the work ahead, actively contribute to and support the work, and help others understand what must happen, how, and why."

"For example," she noted, "one of the potential projects for improving student achievement is 'Development and Implementation of Common Assessments in Each Subject Area at Each Grade Level.' At least one of the schools is not currently working within a team framework, so this initiative will require team-building development as well as scheduling changes to allow teachers to have time to work together on assessments. Teamwork will need to be defined as a performance expectation for the adults in the schools. Performance appraisals will need to include assessment of evidence of teamwork, and all those involved in hiring and assignment of school faculty, administrators, and staff will need to adopt strategies to screen for evidence of teamwork skills when hiring. As you can see, one change initiative requires an entire set of integrated solutions that will engage nearly everyone in every school. One of the schools will require intensive interventions to produce the level of collaboration that will be needed."

examples

"The teams I have been working with during the analysis phase," Chu continued, "are ready to organize the work into a series of improvement projects. Each project will target a defined improvement need with a set of aligned initiatives, or the *hows*, for achieving the results each project will target. Each team working on each project will develop a project commitment agreement, sort of a *project charter* or formal project creation document for each project for you to approve."

Chu worked with the teams on their project commitments, and each principal reviewed his or her teams' completed project commitment agreement with Dr. Rucker and the associate superintendents. After some discussion, the projects were approved. "How do they know what should be done?" one of the associate superintendents asked. "If they knew what to do, wouldn't they already be doing it?"

"That's a good question," Chu replied with a smile. "As we have been conducting the performance and needs analysis, I have been modeling for them the collaborative inquiry and analysis skills that they must use to plan instruction, assessments, and interventions for students together. I have been sharing research with them, and they are working together as learning communities to identify the types of changes and solutions they need to implement. As I am sure you have noticed, in each school, the analysis teams have organized data in the staff workrooms into charts and graphs that reflect assessment, attendance, discipline, teaching observation data, and other types of performance data. We have also developed a model of a standards-based classroom with technology integration at each school. Our shared learning is pointing each team to what they need to do, and we are using project-based learning as the framework for our improvement projects. You will notice that each team developed a driving question for their work. Next, if you are ready to approve that next phase of the work, each team will develop a simple work plan, or project plan. I will guide them through a feasibility scan before they submit their final work plans for your review."

Dr. Rucker and the senior leadership group gave approval for the steps Chu recommended. They scheduled a follow-up meeting ten days later for Chu and the project teams to present their project work plans. Chu coached each team to develop a simple work plan, present their work plan, and field questions. Dr. Rucker and the senior leadership group brainstormed the supports, alignment, and communication needed to support the projects. Chu gained agreement from Dr. Rucker and the senior leadership group to conduct a kick-off meeting to launch each project and to communicate with those who needed to be informed about each project.

A week later, Dr. Rucker and the teams facilitated a kick-off session for each of the projects for all who would be engaged in the work or who needed to know about the project. Later, Chu guided each team to produce an ongoing communication plan for their project and assigned responsibilities for specific individuals to carry out that communication plan. The teams reviewed the Milestone Report that they would be expected to present at each reporting session and agreed to the dates for those reports.

Chu made a calendar of the Milestones Reports and presented it to Dr. Rucker, the principals, and the associate superintendents. "There is one last bit of support we need from you to make these projects successful," Chu said. "We need the expectations for performance by each individual who must contribute to these plans to be clearly communicated by each of you and included in his or her informal and annual performance appraisals. I strongly recommend you have each person who is leading these projects (as well as those who are contributing) develop a project portfolio to collect the evidence of his or her efforts and results. I have some ideas of how to implement those. What do you think? Can I count on your support?"

AN EXAMPLE OF A LESS EFFECTIVE APPLICATION OF STANDARD 4

Faye House was asked by Dr. Henry Cole, the superintendent of the Mill Valley School District, to help his district improve student math scores. Dr. Cole asked House to lead the effort, because she was a certified project manager and was known for her ability to create detailed plans. House began by developing a project overview in which she specified the people and financial resources she required. Her overview included three initiatives: (1) the assessment of teacher's proficiency in math, (2) in-service coaching for teachers of math, and (3) the adoption of course syllabi that included new methods for teaching math concepts. Next, House developed action plans for each initiative. Her action plans were quite detailed and reflected a great deal of thought on her part. Dr. Cole was excited over seeing her work. He announced the start of the projects and passed out the action plans at the next faculty meeting.

REFLECTION

1. What did Chu do that increased the likelihood that the projects needed to close the gaps in performance could be carried out effectively and get the desired results?

2. What did House do—or not do—that could prevent the planned work from being accomplished successfully?

3. What in this chapter might be useful in helping other future improvement projects?

POWER POINTS

Here are some recommendations for planning your school improvement efforts:

- Make use of tools that serve multiple purposes. The tools and worksheets in this chapter and throughout the book are designed to engage others so they become committed to the work. The tools help in the planning and communicating the work being done. They can save you time and reduce the likelihood of missteps, confusion over roles, and conflicts over resources.

• Facilitate others in learning how to use the tools. Ask the team to reflect on the thought processes the tools are designed to invoke. The tools are designed to help the team be diligent in their efforts while being sensitive to the possible impact on future activities and other initiatives.

SUMMARY

Planning a school improvement effort requires buy-in and engagement. The tools in this chapter are designed to help you gain others' input and commitment to the work ahead, specifically in getting their help to

• select the project planning team.
• develop a project commitment statement.
• identify the deliverables.
• break the work to be done down into distinct types of work and the deliverables that are required.
• identify the activities needed to complete those deliverables and place the activities in their logical sequence.
• estimate the required resources.
• estimate the time and costs.
• put together a schedule.
• put together a budget.
• assess the points of risk along the way and how to manage that risk.
• gain the required approvals.

See the end of the book for a complete list of resources and references related to planning.

Additional materials and resources related to
The School Improvement Specialist Field Guide
can be found on the companion website.
http://www.corwin.com/sisguide

Organize and Manage Efforts and Resources

5

Real World Challenge
Bailey's Story, Part 5

"So, how is it going?" Frank Perez asked Bailey Pittman. "Are you making progress?"

"We are!" Bailey said enthusiastically. "Our efforts have good momentum, and the principal and I are working together well. I love this job, but I have never worked so many hours. It can be exhausting. I lay awake every night thinking of all the things that we need to do."

"I know you are doing a great job," Frank encouraged. "Be careful to focus on coordinating the work and guiding those in the school who need to own the work to do it. Don't fall into the trap of doing the work for them. Engage them in thinking through what has to be done and making sure all the needed resources and processes are in place. Break the work down into steps they can follow, and work with the school leaders so they learn how to do what you do. Coach them to organize and coordinate the work. Help them transfer those skills into their day-to-day practice so they will be able to do it independently."

"You are probably right," Bailey admitted. "I am so committed to making them successful that I am taking on quite a bit of the work."

"This week," Frank said, "instead of directing their work, help them write down the next steps they will take, and work with the leaders and team members to make sure their time and resources are organized so that interventions are implemented smoothly. Once they are in control of the work, you can focus on aligning their efforts. If they fully own the work, the likelihood increases that interventions will be sustainable after you leave, and you will be able to sleep better at night."

To be continued . . .

STANDARD 5: ORGANIZE
AND MANAGE EFFORTS AND RESOURCES

As you read in Chapter 4, there are many good training resources available to support mastery of project management. While the technical skills of project management are necessary to be an effective school improvement facilitator, the "softer" skills (such as coaching, giving feedback, and negotiating) are equally critical to getting teams of adults organized and able to implement the plans you have helped them to develop.

Chunking the Work Into Manageable Steps

The first element of Standard 5 reflects your role in helping those you are guiding turn the work into manageable tasks and steps. It is about organizing the work so that others believe it is doable.

5.1 Organize work tasks by breaking them down into feasible steps.

As a facilitator of school improvement, once the interventions are selected and the plans are completed and approved, your challenges are similar to those of teachers who are guiding problem- or project-based learning in the classroom. After students have developed their project plan, the teacher acts as project manager, working with independent teams of students. The teams must break down their projects into manageable parts, organize their work into steps and actions, and then distribute the work and resources among the teams and team members so that the project is completed in time with the intended results. You will play a similar project manager role with the adults you are guiding.

You may be thinking, "We have an action plan (or even a project plan). When can we stop all this planning and get to work?" The answer is *now*. You are now ready to guide teams, organized for each of the various initiatives, into action. A simple tool, a *Task Breakdown Chart*, can be useful in helping your team break the work tasks into steps that can be accomplished by working collaboratively. Figure 5.1 *Task Breakdown Chart, Version A* is an example.

As an expert, you know the work that needs to be accomplished and as a facilitator, you will guide the team members in thinking through their work in advance. Since there will be many tasks to be carried out by different groups, recording the tasks and their related steps and actions will support you later in managing and monitoring the work so that it is well implemented and adequately resourced. An added benefit of doing the task breakdown work is that if you are away from the school, everyone has access to the information to keep the work moving.

Figure 5.1   Task Breakdown Chart, Version A

Task	Steps
Develop common formative assessments for 8th grade science classes.	Define the purpose of the assessment.
	Determine which standards will be assessed and which may be assessed.
	Determine what percentage of each cluster of standards will be assessed.
	Determine what types of test items will be used and in what proportion.
	Select or develop the test items.
	Field-test these items.
	Develop protocols for administration.
	Set cut scores (the score representing the lowest passing score available on a competency test).
	Train/practice scoring.

You can also use a *Task Breakdown Chart* to organize your work in support of the teams. For example, if the team is developing common formative assessments, your task is to facilitate that development effort. Figure 5.2 *Task Breakdown Chart, Version B* illustrates a sample work breakdown for facilitation of that work.

Figure 5.2   Task Breakdown Chart, Version B

Task	Steps
Facilitate development of common formative assessments for 8th grade science classes.	Arrange approved times and a space for meeting.
	Collect resources needed for a development working session.
	Communicate place, time, and prework to team members.
	Develop learning community activities to support assessment development.
	Prepare an agenda for each working session.
	Assign someone to record the group's decisions and next steps.
	Review the timeline and confirm group's acceptance.
	Facilitate the group in deciding how it will work together.
	Facilitate the group as it executes its plan.
	Confirm that the group is on task and can meet targeted deliverable dates.

Tool 5.1   Task Breakdown Chart

Guidelines: To use the *Task Breakdown Chart* for your own work, create a chart similar to the one in Figure 5.1. In the first column, list the task the group wants to accomplish. In the second column, list the steps that have to be taken in order to accomplish the tasks. Where possible, put the steps in a logical order.

Put the task here.	List the steps that must be done to accomplish the task.

Distributing the Work

The second element of Standard 5 is about distributing the duties to those with the appropriate level of control, ownership, and authority.

> 5.2 Effectively distribute work, responsibility and accountability, authority, and leadership so that people are empowered and feel that their time is respected.

At some time in your career, you may have been on the receiving end of a work assignment for which you were accountable for the deliverables and results but lacked the autonomy or power of position you needed. No doubt that was a frustrating experience and one that you must help those you are guiding to avoid. You must support the distribution of the work and leadership of the teams' projects and ensure that each team has enough authority and empowerment to reach its goals. You must also communicate to the team what types of decisions and actions will need approval and which they can undertake autonomously. In his 2009 book, *Drive*, Daniel Pink points to *purpose, autonomy,* and *mastery* as the key elements of motivation for peak performance. Your role is to facilitate achievement of those three powerful performance influencers as you manage the projects the teams are undertaking.

If, early in the process, you helped the team members identify the value they bring to the work at hand, you will have information that will support effective work distribution. Now is the time to help the team determine which task each member is best equipped to lead and to empower those team members to complete those tasks. To extend the example of a team developing common formative assessments, the team would need to establish one person as the leader for the project and divide the work between the members of the team with clear and documented responsibilities and assignments. At this point, it is critical that the team members be engaged in these decisions, so they accept ownership for the work. If not, team members will merely comply rather than invest fully in the change efforts.

Comments such as "Just tell me what to do, and I will do it" are evidence that those you are guiding do not yet own the work. Do not get drawn into the seductive trap of being the "expert" and taking on the team's work as your project. Share the work; do not hoard it. The work ahead is the teams' work, and your job is to get them to do it with passion and a sense of purpose, with full knowledge that ultimately, they will be the ones to reach the targets they set and to achieve their goals or not. Your efforts to build their capacity will help them transfer new skills into practice and achieve the type of mastery that produces engaging work and sustainable results.

Share the work, don't hoard it.

Learning communities and distributed leadership structures are powerful components of schools' improvement efforts. Many good resources exist to guide the development and work of learning communities and the sharing of leadership at all levels. Your role is to determine if the leaders of the school have built a collegial relationship with teachers that allows them to share the leadership, power, and decision-making abilities required to carry out the work they must do together. If not, your work includes facilitating the development of effective learning community processes and distributed leadership by the leaders of the school.

A word of caution: Groups acting as learning communities can get stuck in learning and discussing rather than moving on to informed action. Mastery requires practice and results require action. If you choose to use the powerful process of learning communities or whole-faculty study groups in the suite of interventions for the adults in the school, make sure that the *learning* is an ongoing part of the *doing* that achieves targeted results. If you have been a teacher, at some time you have likely participated in professional development that was not connected to the work you were doing, and your time felt wasted. As the facilitator, you can ensure that the learning you guide is linked to performers' needs and transfers into effective practices and that the precious time of those you are guiding is spent productively.

Here is an example of how one school improvement specialist worked with an assistant principal to appropriately distribute work and build accountability.

Joanne Santoro was assigned to work with middle grade science teachers to improve student performance. Prior to meeting with the teachers, Joanne met with the superintendent, Mrs. Miller, and the principal of the middle school, Mr. Harold, to discuss who should lead this project. Mr. Harold recommended Gwen White, the new assistant principal. Gwen was hired because she had experience as an instructional coach, and he thought it would be a developmental experience for her and the six science teachers at the school. He also thought she would have the authority to arrange for meeting space and to coordinate teacher schedules. Mrs. Miller agreed and added that she wanted Mr. Harold to share the recommendations of the teachers with the other middle schools in the district.

Prior to meeting with the teachers, Joanne met with Gwen. Joanne facilitated the meeting by asking that the two of them take a first cut at putting together a *Task Breakdown Chart* for the initial meeting with the teachers. During the session, Joanne asked specific questions: "What do you see as the main outcome of this assignment? What do you want to better know or understand before meeting with the teachers, and how might you make that happen? How do you see the work being done? What is reasonable goal for the first working session?"

Joanne continued her inquiry to help Gwen mentally rehearse the work ahead. She also wanted to model the type of inquiry she wanted Gwen to exhibit during the meeting.

During the meeting, Gwen shared the *Task Breakdown Chart* and asked the teachers to add any steps they thought were missing. The teachers added the following steps to the *Task Breakdown Chart*:

- Identify and agree on the key learning outcomes.
- Develop and agree on guidelines for assessing the outcomes.
- Match the content to be taught to the outcomes you want to see.
- Identify instructional tactics for teaching the content.
- Create assessment templates that include science problems and questions for each outcome.
- Create guidelines for evaluating the assessment methods.

The teachers also asked about when they would be expected to share their work with other middle grade science teachers in the state to get their feedback. Gwen then asked them how they wanted to work together—as a whole team or individually reporting back to the team. The teachers wanted to start out working together to develop the action plan and later, take responsibility individually for specific tasks, such as how to assess the learning outcomes of the key lessons in the curriculum.

Joanne and Gwen agreed to check in with each other every two weeks to confirm that the project was on schedule and find out what coaching (if any) Gwen might need.

Coordinating and Orchestrating

The third element in Standard 5 is similar to operating as an orchestra conductor—you have to keep an eye on the score while paying attention to the string, percussion, and wind instrument sections so their work is coordinated.

> 5.3 Coordinate efforts, schedules, and human and financial resources in ways that lead to important, agreed-on outcomes with effective stewardship of resources, including time.

While working with the leaders of the school, you will manage the projects and efforts the teams are undertaking. You will need to focus on helping everyone work together. In this case, *managing* means coordinating the work the adults are doing and confirming that they have access to what they need, such as time to work and learn together, access to experts, or tangible assets such as protocols, technology, and other resources needed to carry out their new work. If you have developed a good project plan with milestones, you will be able to purposefully use that plan to coordinate the work so that it stays on track and within budget. Synchronizing the various activities requires thinking through the efforts, working backwards from the various deadlines and checkpoints, and premeditating all that needs to come together to support the work going on in the school.

> You will need to focus on helping everyone work together.

Coordinating a successful project may look effortless to everyone participating, but you will know all the work that went into making it flow smoothly and coordinating the efforts of multiple teams. The *Milestone Report* is a useful tool for keeping track of the progress of multiple teams.

Tool 5.2   Milestone Report

Guidelines: This report is intended to help you document and report information at key points so others are informed of the progress being made, the actions that were taken, and your next steps. It will also help you stay on top of what is and is not being done, so you or the sponsor can intervene if necessary. This report, along with the tools listed in Chapter 4, will provide a document trail of the work that was done, so you and others can learn from it. Go back to the work plan or communication plan your group created and identify what you agreed to report on and when. For each milestone, list the information that was promised. Have the team answer the questions listed below.

Project:	Milestone:
Reporter:	Reported to:

Outcomes: What have been the deliverables and evidence of implementation for this period? *Results*: What has been achieved? (Have capabilities been enhanced, the work improved, or the workplace environment improved?) What are the current levels of measurable performance? *Adjustments*: Using the data and feedback, what changes will be made?
Project Impact: How will the proposed changes impact time, cost, and results? *Approvals:* What changes, if any, are approved?

Sponsor signature: _____ (print) _____

Project facilitator signature: _____ (print) _____

If you are not the person with full authority over the school improvement work, you must work closely with those in charge, supporting their development, gaining access to the needed resources, and coordinating the work. Your job is to help them be successful as leaders of the school and to transfer new skills into practice, just as other team members must do. By modeling the skills that the leaders will use to continue to move the work ahead when you are no longer assigned to the school, you ensure that the new work will stick. Your efforts to bring the school together and carry out the needed work must ultimately manifest itself as the work of the school leaders. Be careful to avoid *taking on* leadership; instead, *build* leadership. Unless the adults in the school have the most critical resource—effective leadership—all of your other efforts will not produce the intended results. If the leaders of the school see you as a valuable resource dedicated to their success, you will have greater access to the resources those you are guiding need to improve performance and results.

Joanne used a project management software program to help her keep track of teams and sub-teams. The software allowed her to look at different levels of data, depending on what she needed at any point in time. For example, she could just look at milestones to identify if any teams were behind schedule. She could also look at each team's action plans to find out if and why they were or were not on schedule. Joanne shared these tools with the leaders of each team. She judged the degree to which the teams were assuming responsibility for the work by observing if and when they asked to create reports, how often they updated information, and if they questioned how to make the plans and reports more meaningful. Joanne wanted Gwen and the other team leaders to become more skilled in using project management tools to help coordinate their work and communicate their progress. She believed that as they became better project managers, they would be better at teaching and supporting their students in managing projects.

AN EXAMPLE OF AN EFFECTIVE APPLICATION OF STANDARD 5

When Derrick Pelman was assigned to his first job as a principal at Elm Hills Middle School, he was excited and a bit anxious after he learned the school held the distinction of being one of the two lowest-performing middle schools in the state. The former principal had retired at the end of the last school year. The faculty and staff had been working with the support of Dr. Nita Abu, a school improvement specialist for two years.

After reviewing the performance data and the plans and work in progress, Pelman held a faculty meeting and introduced Abu as his partner in the improvement of the school. "Dr. Abu will be my guide on the side, and I have no problem with her guiding me. I want her to teach me and tell me what I need to know." He turned to her and said, "Teach, tell, and guide me. Tell me what I should do, and I will decide to do it or not."

Pelham and Abu worked together daily, with Abu breaking down the work ahead into manageable tasks and Pelham leading the school team to carry out the work and sharing key tasks with the leadership team and teachers. While Pelham focused on determining who was "there for the children" or totally focused on helping all students succeed, creating order, eliminating interruptions in the school day, and providing the needed time and resources, Abu helped teachers adopt new practices, collaborate, and learn together.

By the end of the first year of working together, the school had begun to show steady improvement in student performance, morale significantly improved, discipline problems decreased sharply, and attendance of both students and teachers improved by over 40 percent. By the end of their second year of working together, the school met state requirements for the first time.

While speaking to the local newspaper, Pelham recognized Abu, along with the entire school team, for their efforts in the hard work it had taken to reach their goals, "This has truly been a team effort, and Dr. Abu has worked to keep us organized, on task, and learning and getting better day-by-day. Along the way, she transferred her knowledge and skills to all of us, so that we can capably and confidently support our students. We have moved from daily chaos to a stable and engaging working and learning environment."

An Example of a Less Effective Application of Standard 5

Gia Alhambra was pleased with the progress that the school she was assigned was making. Over the last year, she had worked daily to coach teachers in new instructional and assessment practices, and she was beginning to see some of the teachers emerging as leaders in their learning communities. The principal she was supporting was content to let her work with the teachers, and she felt that by doing what came naturally to her, she was helping the teachers improve their practice.

When it was announced that Alhambra was being transferred to another school, the principal and the teachers were reasonably concerned. "How will we do this without you?" they asked. "You know this work so well. What do we do next?"

REFLECTION

1. Think back to a project that you planned and managed using a project plan or other written plan to guide implementation, allocate resources, break down the work into manageable parts, and distribute the work. How did you lay out and manage the project?

What benefits did writing your plan down and following it provide? If you cannot think of a project for which you have used a written plan, why have you not used a written project or action plan?

2. Considering the practices recommended in this chapter, which do you think you could apply to improve your next project?

3. What have you learned from your prior projects that you will apply in managing and guiding future projects?

POWER POINTS

Here are some suggestions about how to do this work:

- Help the group achieve a balance between planning and doing. Planning is not a substitute for doing; and actions without plans may provide a false sense of progress, but they usually waste time and lead to cynicism. Watch to make sure the people do not get burned out through all of the planning and lose energy or interest when it comes to executing the plans.
- You may find that some people are eager and willing to help and that it easier to just let them do it. However, it is important to spread the work among many people. Allow as many people as possible to contribute. Not everyone will contribute to the same level; however, long-term engagement depends on them staying committed to the work. Participating in meaningful work is an important way to sustain engagement.

SUMMARY

This chapter is about how to stay on top of the work and not be a victim of it. Unfortunately, as Bailey was experiencing, you can become overwhelmed by the amount of work to be done. You can also be lured into believing it is easier to do it yourself than to grow the capabilities of others. It is true that in the short term, doing it yourself is easier, but it is very costly in the long term. This chapter has stressed the importance of organizing the work of multiple teams in ways that make the tasks manageable while allowing you to provide oversight, coaching, and help in coordinating their efforts. By staying one step removed, you are in a better position to judge the needs of the people you are working with and to provide the appropriate level of guidance. The next chapter is about building others' capacity to do the work.

See the end of the book for a complete list of resources and references related to organizing work and projects.

Additional materials and resources related to *The School Improvement Specialist Field Guide* can be found on the companion website. **http://www.corwin.com/sisguide**

Guide and Focus Collaborative Improvement

6

"We seem to be at plateau," Bailey Pittman said to Frank Perez. "The teams I have been leading did a really good job in the analysis and planning stages. We have all the plans in place, but I am not sure how to keep everyone engaged and focused on the work and its results. Some people seem to be good at planning, but they are struggling to get started or to be clear about how they will measure their progress."

"Think through the people on the team you have worked with most closely," Frank advised, "and identify those you can directly influence and who they can influence to support the work ahead. If you can keep everyone's eyes and expectations on the work and engage those key supporters, they can help keep people moving in the right direction. What are you planning next?"

"I was thinking of bringing all the teams together in one session, along with a key group of stakeholders, and showing them how to develop their performance targets in the form of SMART goals and how to develop performance metrics," Bailey told Frank.

"That is a good idea," Frank agreed. "Sometimes you also have to help those you are guiding and those who can support their efforts to look back from their plans and targets to the stated values, mission, and vision to make sure that what they are planning reflects what the organization has espoused and endorsed. I have seen this drive revisions and alignment of mission statements, values, or norms and break through issues that may be holding people back from acting with purpose."

"Maybe that can help us get unstuck on one of our key issues," she said. "The organizational mission focuses on preparing students for success in the future, but during the planning process, people have been divided on use of technology. Some people are not sure that having students work online in the classroom with digital curriculum is desirable. Others see that it can support collaboration and develop critical skills. I am planning to use the digital lab during a work session and help the stakeholders see what students can do and how technology can support their own collaboration, learning, and work."

"Keep modeling the way and giving them the information and experiences they need to come to the right conclusions on their own," Frank encouraged. "Elizabeth Moss-Kanter said this of change efforts: 'Everything looks like failure in the middle.' They are not stuck, just going through the phases of the change process. You are working toward a tipping point, where they will decide to make changes, try new practices, and measure their progress with confidence."

To be continued . . .

STANDARD 6: GUIDE AND FOCUS COLLABORATIVE IMPROVEMENT

Whether you are a leader of the school or schools that you are seeking to improve or you are assigned as a performance consultant, you will be successful if you can influence others to take the right actions and make the right decisions. If you have been an effective classroom teacher or another type of high-performing professional, influencing others may come very naturally for you. On the other hand, you may be accustomed to influencing people to let *you do what you know to do* rather than getting *others to do what they need to do.* As an improvement facilitator, you must do both. You need others to trust your judgment, recognize your expertise and deep knowledge of school improvement, and support the interventions you use as a facilitator of performance. They must also follow through on doing the work and implement with fidelity the plans that they helped develop.

Starting With Your Inner Circle

The first element for Standard 6 is about focusing on people who are in your inner circle whose behaviors and decisions are needed to support the work of school improvement.

> 6.1 Influence the behaviors and decisions of stakeholders within a personal circle of influence.

Whether you have direct control and can make the needed actions happen or you must use indirect influence to get others to act, keep in mind that indirect influence may be more likely to result in sustainable action and improvement. The goal is to get people to believe in the course of action and act with purpose, rather than to merely comply.

Successful professionals can be slow to accept the notion that new practices can make them more effective. After all, if they have been successful so far or perceive no negative consequences from their past behavior, why change now? If they have worked solo and achieved what they perceive as the right results, what can they gain from collaborating with others? Changing practices and working with others takes time and effort. If their brains are set to Channel *W.I.I.F.M.* ("What Is in It For Me?"), you may need to point out personal and professional risks and benefits; however, if they are student-focused and purpose-driven, then strategies are needed to connect them to a purpose that yields student outcomes that are more motivating than the status quo.

During your engagement in the school, identify which people you can personally influence and how you could persuade them to do what needs to be done. There are many good resources for learning how to motivate and persuade others, such as Daniel Pink's groundbreaking book, *Drive*, which, as you read in earlier chapters, points to *purpose, mastery,* and *autonomy* as effective adult motivators (Pink, 2009).

It is not possible to fully understand what would motivate every person you are facilitating to change, make tough decisions, or persevere amid challenges. Understanding what his or her motivators would be is helpful, but is not a reliable strategy unless you are a mind reader. The better course of action is to help adults figure things out for themselves so that they have their own "Ah-hah!" moments, which produce new conclusions that cause them to act on their own to change practices. Earlier, you read about the importance of helping adults see the gap between *what they think they know* and *what the facts are.* The first group of adults you need to guide to reach their own conclusions are those you believe have the greatest potential to positively influence others or champion implementation of the planned work.

These guidelines can be useful with those in your personal circle of influence:

1. Engage them in conversations on the improvement you wish to advance by asking questions and listening more than talking.

2. Pre-identify the similarities you have with the person or people you directly engage and make sure that through the conversation, you cover points of parity that strengthen rapport. Conversely, identify the points of difference that make working together and collaborating or cooperating an effective arrangement.

3. Relate stories or use metaphors to create mental images that are persuasive.

4. Avoid using the phrase *have to* or other terms that communicate that someone *should* do something or *should not* do something. Things will rarely turn out exactly as you want or expect. If you

avoid the "you have to do it this way" approach to persuasion and instead facilitate those you are influencing to come to the right conclusions, they are more likely to own and be accountable for the outcomes and results.

5. Focus the conversation on a better outcome that others can support, and be ready to share your ideas (when asked) for specific things your audience can do to contribute to that outcome. Present these as possibilities, not stringent *to-do*s. Invite them to join in inquiry with you to define better ways of reaching goals.

6. Connect to the sense of identity of each person you talk with so that what you need him or her to do reflects his or her unique identity in the context, such as "I am a teacher who other teachers respect," or "I am a person who connects others to resources." (Note: This approach allows you to focus on what you observed a person say or do, rather than trying to guess what is going on between his or her ears that could drive his or her future actions or decisions.)

7. Provide a few vivid details or credible data points and communicate that information as input to help people make up their own minds.

8. Determine what the other person or group wants or needs that you may be able to provide or support while working to meet the needs of the school.

9. Encourage those who you need to participate in or support needed changes so that they feel good about you, themselves, and the possibilities.

For high-priority actions and decisions, you may find a *Roles and Responsibilities Chart* (shown in Tool 6.1) helpful. The chart identifies for each initiative the person or people who will play a role in the initiative and what that role is.

The *Roles and Responsibilities Chart* can be used to identify the people who will play a role in the execution of each task on the action plan. The list below describes typical roles:

- Responsible: List the names of the people who will execute the task.
- Accountable: List the name of the person who has the authority to approve the actions and decisions of the people responsible. Put only one person in this category for each task.

Tool 6.1   Roles and Responsibilities Chart

Task	Responsible	Accountable	Supporters	Guides	Observers
1.					
2.					
3.					

By thinking through who falls in each of these categories, you can begin to determine which of those people are within your direct circle of influence and which are outside it.

- Supporters or sponsors of the work: List the names of the people who you need to be in favor of the work as planned and openly support your actions.
- Guides: List the names of the people who have special expertise or knowledge about how to do the work; these are typically subject matter experts, and they can provide guidance and even help evaluate the work. You want to establish two-way communication with these people.
- Observers: List the people who may not actively participate in the work but who may be affected by it or who can influence outcomes. You want to keep them informed as a courtesy. You want to inform them at the beginning of the benefits of the work and give them periodic updates about the progress of the work, usually at key milestones and at the end of the work.

Reaching Out to a Wider Circle

The second element of Standard 6 is about purposefully expanding your range of influence.

    6.2 Leverage the cooperation and support of others to influence a wider circle of stakeholders.

If you do not have influence over whose support you require or if you do not have a way to effectively communicate with people whose support is needed, identify others who can influence and inform them on your behalf. This type of indirect influence is also needed when you have tried to influence someone directly, but your efforts have not worked because the person or group of people are resistant, highly assertive, or appear disinterested or because influencing directly would be inappropriate.

If you are new to the school or situation you are to influence, find someone with credibility who can introduce you so that you can temporarily borrow some of his or her influence until you can prove your own value, integrity, and credibility. If you are working with a group that is already committed to the change, the *Influence Planner* (Tool 6.2) may help you and the group work together to influence a wider circle.

Tool 6.2   Influence Planner

Guidelines: Work with your sponsor or client to identify who outside your group you want to influence or whose influence you can use. Use the planner to help you think through who the people are, what their position may be on the initiatives you are working on, and how to best work with them.

Who outside our group can influence or impact our success?	What is their position? (circle one)	Who in our group can best communicate with them?	Who outside our group can influence them? Which of us can gain that support?
	○ Resistor ○ Supporter ○ Neutral ○ Other		
	○ Resistor ○ Supporter ○ Neutral ○ Other		
	○ Resistor ○ Supporter ○ Neutral ○ Other		

Consider these questions when determining your ability to influence a wider circle:

- Can you get access to key stakeholders beyond your own group?
- If you need the support of other stakeholders, can you get to the people who can help make this happen?
- When asked to facilitate an improvement project, can you access others who can help you find out how it fits into the larger picture of the school, district, and community?
- When you see an opportunity to make significant improvements, but it requires changing the behaviors of people in other parts of the school, district, or community, can you get to the people who are in a position to champion your idea?
- When you need advice from someone outside your circle of influence, do you know where to get it?

- When you need to know what is *really* going on, do you know who can find out that information?
- Can you effectively identify the official and unofficial flows of power, such as teachers who are highly credible to other teachers, and leverage them?

Look over the lists of people you considered when creating the *Roles and Responsibilities Chart* and the *Influence Planner*. Further sort the people listed by the degree you believe they support the work and are deemed influential by the larger group, as shown in Figure 6.1. Use this new list to set priorities in deciding who to engage first and how to best engage them.

Since your results and your reputation can be impacted by the reputation of those who advocate for you, carefully consider the following:

1. How will the association of your work with this person or organization impact your credibility and reputation? Is this desirable?

2. How well does this person understand what you are doing and why? Do you need to support his or her communication by providing key points in writing? What are the pros and cons of supporting him or her when he or she approaches a person who must be influenced to sponsor or support the work?

Figure 6.1 Influencers Chart

	People More Likely to Support the Work	*People More Likely to Resist or Not Actively Support the Work*
People who have influence or are seen as credible by the larger group	Focus on these people first to get their public endorsement and involvement and their commitment to coach or influence others to support the work.	Focus on this group second to hear and identify ways to address their concerns. Also identify peers they admire who may be supporters and who might help by either engaging this group or minimizing any potential negative effect the group may have.
People who are deemed to have little or no influence over the larger group	Focus on this group third and identify ways to increase their level of influence.	Focus on this group last, even if they are the more vocal of the resisters. Eventually work to get others to help minimize their resistance or change their position.

3. How does this benefit the person who will advocate for you or reinforce how he or she sees themselves (such as "I am an expert in school funding.")?

In general, if you are seeking to build collaborative, cooperative, or coordinated arrangements, have the people who are party to those arrangements

1. discuss and clarify why they are doing this together.

2. define the form of the arrangement. (Is it a partnership? A sponsorship? A shared or distributed work of leadership? Are there other deliberate ways of working together to reach the desired results or benefits?)

3. indicate in writing their agreement with the purpose and the structure of the arrangement and what each will or will not do.

More important, you need to be clear in your purpose: Are you trying to build collaboration or to get people to do work together? Collaborating requires a sharing of vision and purpose that working together does not. If you observe that the adults within the school you are guiding do not share the same ways of thinking about their work or its results, you may need to revisit the performance foundations (the stated mission, vision, values, or beliefs of the school or school district).

Aligning Performance Foundations and Targets

The third element of Standard 6 is about alignment.

6.3 Facilitate the collaborative development of clear mission, vision, purpose, values, goals, and performance targets.

Help adults clearly state the gap between what they say they believe, what they agreed that they want, and how they are acting.

If the actions and decisions of those you are guiding do not match the stated performance foundations, you may need to meet with the group to ask the following questions:

1. Does the current (or proposed) action or decision support the stated mission, vision, values, and goals of the school?

2. What needs to change: the actions or decisions or the statement(s)?

3. Does this action or decision support success for all students? If not, why are we focusing on it?

One common challenge is that people may focus on interventions or programs as "the work" and not clearly define the outcomes and results, how they will be measured, and what will be considered the right results at the end of the measurement period. Deciding how to measure results is a learning process. There are many good resources that help set effective performance measures with the right metrics; one example is Theodore Poister's book, *Measuring Performance in Public and Nonprofit Organizations.*

The process of arriving at good measurements with metrics that gauge progress in meaningful ways requires engaging those who do the work in setting the measures and metrics and refining them over time. For example, is it better to measure the number of days students miss on average or the percentage of students who have over five annual absences? Facilitating discussions about measures and metrics helps clarify what really matters and provides the opportunity to test the performance targets to determine if they reflect what the mission statement intends. For example, if the mission espouses every student achieving success but the targeted graduation rate is less than 100 percent, is the mission statement incorrect or the metric? Does the metric reflect the stated values and beliefs of the organization?

Helping those you are guiding to express their goals in SMART terms is critical to achieving clarity and moving beyond tactical or programmatic focus to a results-based focus. When facilitating others in the development of their SMART goals, use the following questions to guide their work:

S—Specific: Does the goal specifically express what the result will be?

M—Measurable: Does the goal express the measurement and the metric to be applied to assess the results?

A—Attainable: Is the targeted outcome possible within the set measurement period?

R—Relevant: Does the goal and its performance targets align with the direction and purpose of the organization? Can those expected to do the work see the connection between the work and the big picture of the organization?

T—Time-Bound: Is it clear when the work associated with the goal will be checked and the results measured?

Setting SMART goals is no doubt a process you have followed many times, possibly using a formula to express a goal:

The *graduation rate* will *increase* from *78 percent* to *98 percent by 2015.*

In this example, *graduation rate* is the performance indicator; *increase* is the desired change; *78 percent* is the baseline; *98 percent* is the target or goal; and *by 2015* is the time period.

The process of developing a SMART goal is relatively easy, but developing a good one that truly drives performance is an ongoing process that constantly challenges group members to consider what they believe, what they are willing and able to do, and whether they are doing everything possible to achieve the goal. Learning to set the right targets is difficult. Some people rely on guessing, such as "Five percent sounds like a good target." However, setting a target requires knowing why the baseline results are being achieved and what is attainable during the measurement period. Five percent might be a huge stretch or relatively easy. Work with the group to set targets that are based on thorough assessment of performance.

From time to time, you may encounter someone who is hesitant to set a performance target that is challenging. Remember that those you are facilitating may be fearful of the consequences of not meeting every target. Remind them that the target is just that—a target to guide efforts. They are unlikely to reach every target and are likely to exceed some targets. Coach leaders and leaders' supervisors to use the targets to monitor progress and coach performance rather than to blame or punish. You will focus on this more deeply in the next few chapters.

Providing Relevant Information

The fourth element of Standard 6 is about providing information and guidance that people value and can use to succeed in making needed changes.

> 6.4 Provide relevant information and advice to support improvement, transformation, and sustainability.

As you guide the adults through the improvement and transformation process, your value will be assessed in part by the usefulness and quality of the information you provide. Cultivating a network of peers who have experience in helping facilitate positive changes and enduring results in schools is key to accessing the type of information and advice you need along the way.

If you actively monitor what researchers have found, conduct collaborative action research with others who are engaged in this work, and share your findings, you will generate a repository of information and ideas that can support your practice as an effective performance consultant. The electronic portfolio and the social networking tools provided to applicants of the Certified School Improvement Specialist certification (through the International Society for Performance Improvement, in partnership with Accredited Portfolios, Inc.) provides storage for your information, evidence of your effective practice, and connects you virtually to peers engaged in school improvement work. Even if you are not pursuing certification, the electronic portfolio can be a powerful tool for organizing and sharing information, demonstrating your proficiency, and collaborating with others. You can learn more at http://www.accreditedportfolios.com.

Helping schools improve test scores may be part of your role, but helping those who work in schools and stakeholders to reimagine education to meet future needs is both worthy work and relatively uncharted territory. If your research includes learning about educational processes and policies that can change schools so they meet students' needs now and in the future, you will be better equipped to facilitate those changes. The facilitative processes that you have been focusing on in this book support not only achieving incremental and steady improvements but also the creation of breakthrough interventions that will allow schools to meet ever-changing needs and expectations.

A common challenge in standard school strategic planning processes is that they take input from stakeholders, whose vision may be limited to the mental model of what schools were in their past or who are too narrowly focused on the students they know best. Their perceptions of current and future job markets, economic conditions, and global challenges impact their vision. Limited or uninformed visions will not produce effective strategic plans and will not move schools ahead to be relevant to the needs of their students now or in the future.

To facilitate breakthroughs and innovation, you must ask, "How big is the vision? Is it rooted in pursuit of what schools can be, rather than what they have been?" At the time of this writing, there are numerous books that guide inquiry into the types of schools and skills students will need in the future, including *21st Century Skills: Learning for Life in Our Times* by Bernie Trilling and Charles Fadel and *21st Century Skills: Rethinking How Students Learn,* edited by James Bellance and Ron Brandt.

The key stakeholders who must deepen and expand their thinking to create a relevant vision for their schools are the school board, school governance teams, and district governance teams, including school leadership teams. As a school improvement specialist, your role is to influence thinking at every level to result in relevant, sustainable plans focused on the best results that can be imagined for each student the school serves. Providing updates on issues relative to schooling now and in the future, job and skills forecasts, and information regarding innovations and their results can help those who govern, lead, and support schools to expand their thinking about what must be done to help schools meet students' needs and community needs. The Center for Public Education (http://www.centerforpubliceducation.org) provides relevant reports and research, as do the Wallace Foundation, Bill & Melinda Gates Foundation, The Aspen Institute, The Buck Institute, KnowledgeWorks, and many others.

Your role is to help each group of stakeholders determine what meaningful work they can do individually and collectively to advance the school or schools toward the vision of what they can achieve. You must help them select interventions (such as policies) that ensure that changes in leadership will not change the direction of change and improvement. The selected interventions must work together to sustain efforts, directions, and results with a persistence of vision that supports enduring success for all. Not a small job!

Being an intentional connector between the purposes and practices that have been used in the past and those that can contribute to future success will support the change process. Your role is to guide change by honoring what has been *and* supporting the creation of what can be. Appreciative inquiry practices are extremely useful in this effort. The resource section at the end of this book contains suggested books and tools for appreciative inquiry, including identifying the positive core of the school or schools you serve, dreaming of an ideal future state built from that positive core, designing that future, and working together to deliver the imagined state and results.

5 Modeling the Right Behaviors

The fifth element of Standard 6 is about modeling the behaviors you want to see in others.

> 6.5 Model the behaviors of continuous improvement and 21st-century transformation.

The best way to facilitate others in mastering the processes of continuous improvement and the types of thinking and actions that help schools reinvent themselves for better outcomes for students is to model those practices and share how you challenge yourself and others to learn and change. If you model the best methods available, you will be able to develop the types of skills and deep knowledge in yourself and those you are guiding to solve the problems of the present and future.

To help others, you must constantly expand and deepen your expertise. Consider the following:

- On what topics do you have knowledge relative to school improvement and 21st-century school transformation?
- Are you an expert in this field and continuous learner?
- What are you learning from your daily practices?
- Are you reflecting on your progress and expertise and seeking ways to improve what you do and what students need to do to be successful in the future?
- Are you modeling that for others?

Your goal is to help those you guide—not as a gatekeeper, but as a knowledge broker. If you model this role, you can help others shift from being managers to being agents of learning and performance improvement. If you desire those you guide to learn together, you must model and establish a broader learning environment, where problems are continuously being solved and innovations are evolving. If those you are guiding see you support learning anywhere, anytime, just enough, just in time, and at the point of need, it will be easier to imagine and support changes in school that allow the same process for students.

L.C. (Buster) Evans is a Certified School Improvement Specialist and superintendent of a school system that is making solid progress toward transformation of schooling to meet 21st-century needs.

As we monitor the use of our online tools and resources, we have found that the prime time in which most learning occurs in our community is 8:00 in the evening. The change to expand . . . learning beyond the classroom and [beyond] the span of a traditional school day is gradually taking hold here.

My biggest challenge has been convincing adults—including family members of our students—that school doesn't have to look like it has in the past to be effective. After all, in the current digital and knowledge age, our students live in a world where they are highly connected, and old borders and boundaries are dissolving. Our students can master Mandarin Chinese, even though no one in our system teaches it. We have found the external resources to provide that learning effectively and efficiently. Our students can connect with and learn with peers and experts around the globe. Just as supply chains circle the globe and involve many different people in many places, global learning is happening the same way. We must leverage and support that [global learning] for our students and those who work in our schools to succeed in the future.

Those of us who lead and guide these types of changes have to model the skills our students need to be successful. As leaders of a community of schools, we need to be adept at creating networks and partnerships that result in our schools becoming vibrant learning [centers] and service centers for our communities, with the support of our community members and organizations. (L.C. Evans, personal communication, October 2, 2011)

Evans and those who work in the school district he leads must consider and continuously ask the following questions:

- What do we want for our students?
- Is the education we are providing as good as it can be?
- Will the education we provide result in our students having the expertise for successful work, family, and community lives?
- Are we developing ourselves and our students as lifetime learners?
- Will our efforts improve the quality of life for our students and our community?
- What will success look like?

Taking on the Hard Decisions

The last element of Standard 6 is about helping stakeholders make the needed tough decisions.

> 6.6 Facilitate or influence tough decisions needed to achieve needed changes and breakthroughs.

The types of questions Evans, his team, and the community are asking are compatible with a central premise of Appreciative Inquiry: "Organizations and people move in the direction of that which they persistently ask questions about." Getting people to make tough decisions to support needed changes doesn't always require focusing on problems and what is broken. Instead, elevate inquiry to be aspirational in focus so that you can move people past where they are stuck.

You can help others think like experts by guiding them to see trends and patterns, connecting them to knowledge and others with expertise and similar experiences, and teaching them what they need to know to choose the best interventions for the issues and opportunities at hand.

Tackling tough decisions, even unpopular ones, need not be an unpleasant part of your role. If you have developed enough expertise in others for them to effectively diagnose gaps and problems and select interventions, they will be able to take pride in their tough decisions and effectively defend their choices.

AN EXAMPLE OF AN EFFECTIVE APPLICATION OF STANDARD 6

Rashana Pillar was pleased with the plans the schools she was guiding had developed and the way they had organized the work, their time and resources, and themselves to carry out their plans. At first, some of the leaders in the schools had been anxious about using shared leadership processes, which included students' family members, community leaders, and central office staff along with teachers and leaders in each school. Pillar shared research with the principals and superintendent and organized a visit to a school district that had been using distributed structures and authority successfully.

Getting the cooperation and support of a broader group of stakeholders required Pillar to work with the superintendent to engage the director of professional development, members of the local community foundation, the parent-teacher association, a representative of the chamber of commerce, clergy members, and a public relations expert who was willing to volunteer some time to work with the groups to communicate their plans and their progress.

Bringing the wider circle of stakeholders into the improvement process required Pillar to facilitate working sessions with the superintendent, school board, and transformation councils that they formed within the school to support the implementation of the plans that had been developed. Pillar facilitated a workshop with the superintendents and the councils, bringing them up-to-date on research and issues relative to preparing students for success in their future world of work and community and family life. The groups completed assessments, reviewed the performance foundations of the school district, and reviewed the plans and performance targets to determine their degree of alignment to the stated mission and values of the district. Pillar used the same processes a teacher would use in a project-based assignment to facilitate the retreat. After reflecting on the experience through a lively discussion, the groups determined that they wanted to model the types of skills students needed to acquire in their working sessions.

One board member summed up the conclusions the group had reached as "Until now, as stakeholders, we have sat back and made sure our schools were well managed and compliant. Now we see that there is meaningful work that we need to do to support our schools as they make the kind of changes needed to move our students ahead in the 21st century. Our role includes bringing our community along to support the changes that need to be made. Let's face it—school over the next 50 years will look nothing like it did in the last 50 years. We need to make some big changes, and we cannot expect these schools to do this work without our support and sponsorship."

AN EXAMPLE OF A LESS EFFECTIVE APPLICATION OF STANDARD 6

Getty Tills works in the central office of a school district with twelve schools. Her role is to guide the leadership teams in each school to continuously improve their schools. The principals report directly to the superintendent, not to Tills. After guiding the leadership teams through analysis and intervention selection and plan development, she worked with them to form teams within their schools and some cross-functional teams between schools to focus on systemic issues the leaders had identified. Each team had developed simple action plans and divided the work to be completed. The principals presented their teams' goals to the superintendent and school board along with what they were committed to achieve by the end of the school year.

The day following the presentations, the superintendent met with Tills. "I enjoyed their presentations, but I kept thinking, 'How committed are they to this, and how are they going to measure their performance?' I saw lots of projected outcomes, like setting up partnerships with the local university for teacher preparation and developing a hiring process that is more inclusive of school leadership teams. I did not see measures of performance or any intentions to include all the stakeholders needed to accomplish their goals. I sensed that the team members were anxious about sharing leadership and authority. One of our core values is engagement. What do you think is missing in this process?"

REFLECTION

1. What did Pillar do that guided and focused collaborative improvement?

2. What did Tills do or not do that reduced confidence that the efforts and results will be sustainable?

3. What in this chapter will be useful in your future facilitation of collaborative efforts, especially those in which people may be divided on how to accomplish a goal?

POWER POINTS

Here are some suggestions about how to do this work:

- Network with other school improvement specialists. Post questions to your network about how to achieve real engagement by the stakeholders. Ask how they facilitate conversation about what metrics to use that are aligned with the mission, vision, and values of the school. Set up exchanges where you can discuss techniques they and you have used and what the outcomes were.
- Be sensitive to protecting your reputation and pay attention to the reputation of others. Think of your reputation as an intangible asset. In addition to how you behave, the value of your reputation is affected by who you know, who you associate with, and who you are afforded access to. Handle it carefully. Once your reputation is lost, it is very difficult to reclaim.

SUMMARY

This chapter builds on the ideas presented in Chapter 5 by stressing the importance of building and nurturing relationships with all of the stakeholders, whose support will be essential to improving performance of students, teachers, and leaders and then sustaining those improvements long term. This chapter focuses on how to use your political savvy, so you can build and leverage professional relationships without sacrificing your personal integrity or feeling like you are using others. It starts with you working from the known (the people you trust and who trust you) then moving into the less known (engaging people with whom you initially have less in common). The standard discussed in this chapter requires you to model the right behaviors that include expanding your sphere of influence, staying current in the research, and asking the hard questions.

See the end of the book for a complete list of resources and references related to collaboration.

Additional materials and resources related to
The School Improvement Specialist Field Guide
can be found on the companion website.
http://www.corwin.com/sisguide

Build Capacity   7

When Bailey Pittman checked her voicemail, she was pleased to hear the voice of Frank Perez. "I haven't heard from you in a while. You are so good at teaching and leading others; I know you are doing great work. Give me a call when you have time to catch up."

When Bailey returned his call, she said, "It was so nice to hear your message. You always encourage me. You mentioned teaching others. Sometimes I wonder who is learning more—the people I am trying to help or me. When I was a principal, I knew my team and my school so well that much of what I did came naturally. I didn't have to think about it that much. Knowing that I am assigned to help others do the work and to transfer my capacity to them is causing me to constantly look for new techniques to be more effective as I teach them and guide them."

"I know what you mean," Frank said. "Over the last five years, I have immersed myself in learning and applying a systematic approach to improving the accomplishments of administrators, teachers, and staff. What I have learned is that professional learning is a vital part of building the competency of those I serve; however, for their learning to transfer into good on-the-job performance, I must develop and model other types of interventions that support transfer of learning into practice and help them build the confidence to do it themselves."

"I am very interested in learning all I can about methods for helping people perform at their highest level," Bailey said. "As a principal, I had a chance to impact the talent on my team through hiring and assignment; I could choose who to hire and where to place them. Now, I am working with the principal to think about how selecting teachers and staff impacts results and to focus on building the capacity of the team he has. There is some great talent and potential in the school, but much of it is untapped and undeveloped, and some people are not in the right roles."

"I know what you mean," Frank agreed. "I had a basketball coach back in college who once told me, 'Frank, you cannot teach height. Some people just have what it takes to be effective in a given position.' I think about that sometimes when I am working with the wide range of performers in a school. They bring their unique strengths and their unique needs. To extend the metaphor, getting the right people with the right strengths on the team and playing in the right position is critical, but we also have to meet each person where he or she is and coach them to where he or she can be. Feedback is critical, as is reflection, meaningful and effective evaluation, and a culture where learning and risk taking are encouraged."

"I am approaching the work I am doing as action research," Bailey said. "I am devouring every resource available on developing adults' performance. I try new techniques and reflect in my journal in my electronic portfolio. Every day, I feel like I learn more and become a bit more effective. My latest insight is that the current evaluation process is not supporting improvement. I have to figure out how to address that."

"I have worked on improving evaluation, and I can connect you to a couple of colleagues who have done that successfully," Frank offered. "I will call you next week and arrange time for us to talk."

"Thanks, Frank," Bailey said. "I am convinced that a better interim and annual evaluation process is needed, and I want to ask all of you some questions about how you influence more effective selection and assignment processes. I look forward to it."

To be continued . . .

STANDARD 7: BUILD CAPACITY

One of the ironies of school improvement is that those who are expected to develop the capacity of other adults in schools rarely have been provided training in designing and delivering adult learning and performance interventions. Likewise, it is unusual for teachers to have formal training in instructional design. Expectations are growing for students to not only learn content and demonstrate their knowledge on tests but also to perform tasks that demonstrate their ability to transfer their knowledge into action. The change to more problem- and project-based instruction requires teachers to be effective instructional designers. In turn, those who train and develop teachers and other educators must be effective designers of the types of interventions that allow learning to transfer into practice and practice to produce the right outcomes and outputs.

Using Effective Adult Interventions

The first element of Standard 7 is about how to develop the capacity of adults.

> 7.1 Use effective adult learning and performance interventions aligned to the desired outcomes and results.

If you have determined that learning and performance interventions are needed to build the capacity of those you are facilitating, you can ask these questions to help you design those interventions to build adults' capacity:

1. What goal will the performer achieve or support achieving? (For example: The teacher will help all students to achieve proficiency on the standards they are taught.)

2. What outcomes, outputs, and work products will the performer produce that will provide evidence of proficiency? (For example: Those assessing teacher performance can look at a variety of student test scores, student work with teacher and peer commentary, data from teacher observation of students' performance on assigned tasks that demonstrates their knowledge and mastery of specific standards, lesson plans with activities and tasks, teaching observation ratings and observer notes, student engagement ratings, and the safety of the environment in which students perform.)

3. What will the performer do on the job as a result of the new or enhanced capacity? (For example: After a professional development session, at the beginning of lesson, the teacher will provide a pretest and divide students into flexible groups based on the data from the pretest. The teacher will then provide the students with a variety of resources to support their performance of an assigned task and provide a choice of ways in which the students can demonstrate their learning.)

4. What capacity must be developed or enhanced?

   a. What skills must the performer master to perform that work effectively? (For example: The teacher must maintain order in the classroom, develop pretests, develop the performance task, plan, use time wisely, sort students into various groups, develop an activating strategy to engage students, access resources for instruction, facilitate learning, and so on.)

   b. What knowledge does the performer need to perform that work effectively? (For example: The teacher must know what effective differentiation is, understand the practices required to differentiate instruction in the classroom, and be knowledgeable about the content in the curriculum, the standards, and the available sources of resources for students.)

5. How often will the performer need to perform the work? (For example: When students in the classroom are at different levels of mastery, the teacher will use his or her skills to move each student from his or her current level of mastery to a higher level of mastery.)

6. Why is doing the work important? (For example: Differentiation of instruction creates engagement and makes learning more student-centered and more likely to be recalled in the long term.)

7. What factors in the work context can impact performance, and what must the performer do to perform effectively in that context? (For example: The students must be engaged to participate in the learning, so the performer will need to plan and use some type of activating strategy that creates engagement in the lesson and its content. The teacher must also make time for planning, time for the instruction, and so on to effectively prepare for the lesson.)

8. What resources does the performer need? (For example: The teacher must have a clear understanding of the standards; books, articles, and websites for students to use; a classroom with movable furniture for grouping; etc.)

9. How will the performer know that it is time to do the work? (Example: The teacher can look at preassessments to see which students in the classroom are at different levels of mastery.)

By thinking through these questions before designing instruction, you can design and develop training and instruction that can transfer into effective practice on the job. Begin by writing the *performance objectives* for the adults you are teaching and training. A performance objective includes a verb that defines what the performer will be able to do as a result of the training or performance intervention. It does not describe a cognitive function such as *understand, compare, synthesize,* or *know,* even though those functions may be performed in support of applying what has been learned in practice. An example of a performance objective is "The teacher will *assess* students' mastery through a pretest." However, a *learning objective* describes what must be taught; an example of a learning objective is "how to develop a pretest to assess student mastery."

Assessment of the performance will indicate whether or not performance criteria were met. An assessor must judge if an individual can perform a specific activity to the performance criteria, which are standards set in advance for the work. This means that before you can design and develop capacity-building interventions, you must develop the performance objectives and the related performance criteria. From there, you can develop learning objectives for the knowledge and skills that the performer will need.

There are many good resources for guiding design and development of adult learning and training. The Center for Effective Performance at http://cepworldwide.com/ provides courses and resources for mastering the development of performance-based training using the types of questions provided earlier in this chapter.

A challenge in capacity building is determining the most efficient and effective way to help those you are guiding to reach competency as quickly as possible. The often-used solution for closing performance gaps is providing training, but performers may do just as well with job aids or protocols that guide them at the moment of need to perform tasks. This type of "just enough and just in time" support is useful for important tasks that are performed infrequently or that are complex and hard to recall. An example might be how to correctly report how many full-time students attend the school or how funds for a specific grant can and cannot be used. In some cases, both training and job aids may be needed. There are some good resources available for learning to develop job aids, protocols, and performance support tools in the resources section at the end of this book.

Learning communities are capacity-building interventions often applied in schools. Robert Eaker and Richard and Rebecca Defour's book, *Revisiting Professional Learning Communities at Work,* is an excellent resource for supporting learning communities, in which adults learn and work together toward a common improvement goal.

In general, as the facilitator, your role is to:

- create time and space for the adults to learn and work together and to collaborate and reflect on their practices together.
- focus on a specific topic relating to an improvement goal.
- determine in advance what you want people to know and be able to do as a result of participating.
- provide resources, especially research, to support learning and guide practice.
- break the learning and practice into small manageable chunks of work that you can teach step-by-step.
- model the practices that the adults need to do and give them opportunity to practice.
- help the adults form commitments for what they will do on the job using their new or enhanced capacity.
- observe the adults applying the new practices and provide feedback.
- repeat the process until the adults have successfully applied what they have learned on the job and have evidence of effective practice, outcomes, results, and goal achievement.

Your role is to model effective learning community facilitation, but the primary goal is transferring your capacity to the others who will continue to do the work (and do it well) long after you are no longer guiding the work. Rather than leading a learning community, you must support and coach others to lead it, giving feedback and coaching them as needed. Thomas Van Soelen is an associate superintendent in a city school district that consistently performs above national standards. He is a Certified School Improvement Specialist who is also certified to facilitate Critical Friends Groups through the School Reform Initiative. A *Critical Friends Group* is a professional learning community of educators who come together regularly to improve their practice through collaborative learning. Van Soelen reflects on the process of effective facilitation:

> Becoming an effective facilitator requires focusing on facilitation as a process that requires commitment, unlearning of old habits, and mastering new practices. One must claim facilitation as a skill that is important to master, practice the skill every day, and model, model, model for others. Good facilitation requires harnessing the power of questions and being open to giving and receiving descriptive feedback. I particularly find it helpful to co-facilitate with another trained facilitator so we can observe each other, reflect together, and give each other feedback to improve our craft as facilitators. (T. Van Soelen, personal communication, December 5, 2011)

Coaching and Giving Feedback

The second element of Standard 7 describes more directly what your role is in building capability.

7.2 Coach and provide feedback against clear criteria.

If you develop performance objectives and performance criteria for the work you are teaching and supporting, you will be able to communicate the performance expectations to others and share with them the criteria for success. Like students in the classroom, adults need to know how they will be assessed and what criteria will be applied. Communicating performance standards and criteria before an adult attempts new work allows that performer to know exactly what will be inspected and how good is good enough.

Your role as a coach is similar to that of a personal trainer, who helps people master specific exercises to strengthen and improve physical strength, flexibility, and health. You cannot teach and support everything a principal, teacher, or staff member needs to be able to do. Instead, prioritize the practices within the body of work each adult must master. Assess and help each performer to self-assess how well he or she is performing those tasks on the job. Share and compare ratings on a performance continuum from *beginning* to *developing* to *proficient* to *role model*. Your role is to move each adult from where they are to where they need to be by teaching, coaching, and giving specific feedback against clear, predefined performance criteria for each new task or practice.

Eventually, you will encounter someone who you are training and coaching who is not transferring the new practices into his or her work. If the person has practiced the work with your oversight and you have determined that he or she *can* do the new work and meet the performance standards but is choosing not to, your coaching must become very specific about what the performer is or is not doing and the consequences of nonperformance to the individual, those he or she is leading or teaching, and to the overall organization. Ferdinand F. Fournies' book, *Coaching for Improved Work Performance* (2000), is an excellent guide for analyzing performance factors and handling tough performance conversations. Fournies points to the importance of helping each person who is underperforming to understand the consequences of underperformance and guides supervisors to recognize how they hurt themselves when they fail to address the underperformance of those who work for them. In your role you must determine if the causes of underperformance are under the control of the performer or the supervisor or the organization. If you analyze the work, workers, and workplace, you are likely to find barriers outside the performer's control or motivators for nonperformance. Your role as coach is to work with the individual's supervisor to address barriers and motivate effective performance.

Asking Questions

The third element Standard 7 is about a key part of the coaching process: helping the adults you are serving to reflect on their own practice. You will guide them in asking questions relating to what is working well, why they are or are not doing what they have learned to do, or how they can be more effective in their on-the-job performance.

> 7.3 Ask questions that cause reflection so that others surface new possibilities and recognize self-imposed barriers.

There are opportunities throughout the process of facilitating others in doing the work to help people improve their practices by asking the types of questions that support critical reflection. John Dewey defined the education process as a "continual reorganization, reconstruction, and transformation of experience" (1938, p. 50). Your role is to help others learn by reflecting on their experience and extracting meaning that will inform their future actions and decisions.

Certified School Improvement Specialists (CSIS) develop a portfolio of evidence aligned to each of the ten CSIS standards. Not only does the electronic portfolio store evidence of proficiency and results, it also provides a structure for an individual specialist to reflect systematically over time on his or her practices and to develop the skills, habits of mind, and capabilities that come from critical reflection and that support lifelong learning and investigation.

> We do not learn from experience . . . we learn from reflecting on experience (Dewey, 1938, p. 78).

David Kolb (1984) developed *The Learning Cycle* to represent a process that results in learning with real comprehension and the transfer of knowing into doing:

- Have an experience.
- Reflect on the experience.
- Learn from the experience.
- Try out what you have learned.

By applying this process with those you are coaching and in your own practice, you can exponentially improve performance, outcomes, and results. Reflection is particularly useful in supporting learning and performing work that addresses ill-structured, messy, and complex problems with no clear-cut answers. As you coach others, your role is to create challenging assignments and experiences that target a specific result and goal as well as a safe, supportive environment for reflection.

As you coach and facilitate reflection, plan tasks that challenge the adults to integrate new learning into prior knowledge and that require them to order their thoughts and to self-evaluate their work against the performance criteria. By helping them order their thinking and practice, both their theories and their practice are made explicit. As they reflect and think about what they are thinking when they take certain actions or make decisions, you help them achieve the type of higher-order thinking skills or metacognition that allows them to extract learning from their work to inform their future practice (Moon, 1999).

Figure 7.1 provides sample questions that you can use to guide reflection as you train and coach others.

Figure 7.1   Examples of Reflective Questions

1. What were you attempting to do?

2. Were you able to do it well?

3. What materials and skills did you use based on what you have recently learned? How effective were they?

4. What specific techniques did you use?

5. What happened?

6. Did you do anything differently than you have in the past?

7. Did you encounter any problems along the way?

8. What were you thinking as you did this, and what decisions did you have to make?

9. Did you have to do something differently than you had planned? If so, what and why? Did it work better or worse?

10. What was the most successful part? What was the least successful part?

11. What did you accomplish?

12. If you did this again, would you do it the same way? What changes would you make?

13. Did you discover anything about your practices and performance?

14. How did those you were guiding or teaching respond?

15. What did others do that you wanted them to do? What did they do that you would not want to happen again?

By developing questions and conducting regular reflection sessions throughout the learning and performance cycle, you can guide those you are facilitating to work through complex challenges step-by-step and to draw meaning from their experiences to inform future actions and decisions.

One of the most critical processes that can draw upon structured experiences and reflection is the induction or transition of individuals into new jobs or new roles. Effective induction practices include but are not limited to the following:

- handbooks and job aids
- structured assignments with clear, preset performance criteria

- performance feedback against the performance criteria
- a peer group or network of other inductees
- a group or network of support by more expert performers, who model the expected behaviors and practices
- professional development plans aligned to the current or next assignment
- on-the-job performance coaching
- coaching with reflection on performance and goal setting
- training and development
- identification and support for addressing performance barriers outside of the inductee's control
- structured mentoring by a compatible peer mentor
- support in navigating operational processes, such as how to order resources
- structured orientations
- access to a performance coach, professional developer, or other designated supporting individual
- access to resources for development

As a school improvement specialist, you will find that performance portfolios are excellent resources for inducting new or transitioning performers, building capacity, and improving performance. These tools help you to

- guide reflection on practice.
- coach performance.
- assess gains in capability and performance.
- support sharing of practices.

If you pursue CSIS job certification, you will experience firsthand the benefits of using an electronic portfolio. You will use the electronic portfolio provided with your application to document your practice and store evidence of proficiency in each of the CSIS standards as well as the outcomes and results of your work. The networking and sharing tools within the portfolio will allow you to form groups with colleagues, collaborate with others on improvement initiatives, and put forward either evidence of your evolving practice or your best evidence of your expertise and performance. As you become effective in using the portfolio within your practice, you will be able to model portfolios as powerful tools for administrators, teachers, staff, students, and even members of the school or district governance team.

Dr. Sally J. Zepeda, professor in the Department of Lifelong Education, Administration, and Policy at the University of Georgia, points to the value of portfolios in formative and summative evaluation.

> The portfolio allows school leaders to work with teachers over an extended period of time due to the formative aspects of developing the artifacts to include in the portfolio. Given the ongoing assessments that teachers make while making decisions about what to include in the portfolio, the teacher emerges as a self-reflective professional who is able to make decisions about practices that can improve teaching and learning. (S. Zepeda, personal communication, December 28, 2011)

Facilitating Study

The fourth element of Standard 7 delves deeper into the practice of facilitating learning and building capability.

> 7.4 Facilitate study, inquiry, and informed action that address complex challenges while working effectively with colleagues.

One of the main advantages of learning communities is that they allow adults to learn, think, plan, dream, and design collaboratively. Together, they can identify and improve processes and practices; unravel mysteries; and maintain alignment as they tackle complicated problems. Part of your job is to help the adults to embrace their new role as continuous learners and to embrace the importance that learning plays in continuous improvement. This requires breaking the mindset, established during adults' experiences in their own schooling and preparation, that learning occurs separately from working.

Learning Forward (formerly the National Staff Development Council) adopted standards for professional development that define job-embedded learning as key to improving educators' performance. *Job-embedded* does not only mean that the adults are provided with protected time to study, learn, and inquire together but also that they individually incorporate inquiry and learning into their unique, individual daily practice to the end of solving problems and producing observable outputs, outcomes, and improved results. Day-to-day demands can easily sidetrack those you are facilitating. Even though the problems they face are complex, you can help by guiding those you are working with to focus on each of the interdependent performance factors that are producing the current results and by providing job aids or scaffolds to help them study and address each

Figure 7.2   Guiding Questions

1. What single, specific gap in performance within *my* control am I trying to close?

2. What is happening? What are the results of what is happening?

3. What *could be* happening? What results do I want?

4. What do I have to do next to close that gap?

5. What resources have I used to identify and master what I have to know and be able to do in order to be effective in closing the gap?

6. What are the criteria for effective performance?

7. Did I do it effectively?

8. Repeat the questions.

factor systematically. Facilitate those you are guiding to premeditate independently and, ideally, with you or a peer before they perform. Figure 7.2 lists a series of questions designed to help others stay focused on how to continually learn.

By working through this simple set of questions and repeating the questions after each on-the-job performance you are coaching, you can help others focus, one step at a time, on their practice without being overwhelmed by the complexities of that practice.

Guiding action research in learning communities is another way that you, as the improvement facilitator, can guide a disciplined cycle of inquiry and action. The process will help you and the people you are coaching to stay focused on their personal practice, the group's performance, and the schools' performance. When the process creates intentional awareness of practices, processes, and performance, the likelihood that changes and improvements will be sustained increases. If group members recognize each other as coresearchers working together to discover what works, they develop a deeper shared commitment to finding answers and refining practices. Your role is to help them purposely move from being an individual learner and performer to a contributor to the group's work and back again.

Action research can support scholarly research and has the advantage of capturing the *knowing* that results from inquiry and practice and using that knowing to improve performance and results. While scholarly research reveals the underlying theoretical foundations of actions and decisions, action research informs adoption and documentation of improved practices that achieve targeted results and support sharing of learning and improved practices. Action research is especially helpful in growing people's capability to address complex problems, especially the types of problems facing schools today.

Facilitating Sharing

The fifth element of Standard 7 is about sharing what is learned so others can benefit.

> 7.5 Facilitate sharing of learning that leads to improved practices, innovation, and positive change.

Part of your job is getting the adults who work in schools to share what they have learned with others so that this new knowledge is applied to solving problems and getting the right work done. This new knowledge becomes the knowledge base of the organization. One way of thinking of your role is to be the knowledge manager, helping to make others' implicit know-how that gets the right results explicit so that it can be taught to others and sustained.

The International Society for Performance Improvement (http://www.ispi.org) has adopted the tagline *Where Knowledge Becomes Know-How.* You may think of your learning community as your context for doing the same. Your role is to help people transfer what they learn into practice; refine and codify those practices; and share them with others so that together they can create solutions and breakthroughs and invent the future state of their school.

A learning management system (LMS) can provide the architecture and technology on a web-based platform for managing and delivering the growing knowledge of the organization and for using it and other knowledge-based resources (training programs, online events, e-learning programs, and training content) to teach adults and support their performance. An LMS supports and automates administration, documentation, tracking, and reporting and allows both self-service by performers and guided services. Learning content can be stored in the system for easy access and reuse.

As schools explore and implement digital curriculums, an LMS will support implementation for students. Those systems will be useful for supporting adult learning and performance, too. If the school or school system you support has not yet implemented a digital curriculum or LMS, you would still do well to learn about them so that you can align your work with adults with the systems implemented to support students. Lissa Pijanowski, EdD, former Associate Superintendent at Forsyth County Schools, shared her experience with using an LMS:

> We have leveraged our learning management system to create a one-stop shop for shared resources for curriculum, instruction,

and assessment as well as a place to facilitate collaboration and professional learning for our adult learners. Building the capacity of the professional educators in our organization leads to improved performance and learning for all. (L. Pijanowski, personal communication, December 14, 2011)

Facilitating Adoption

The final element of Standard 7 is about facilitating the adoption of new practices by others to support and sustain the results that come about through improved practices.

> 7.6 Facilitate adoption of defined and aligned practices in hiring, selection, assignment, development, and formative and summative performance evaluation that support improved performance of teachers, administrators, and staff.

You can spend countless hours and endless resources on the adults who lead, teach, and carry out the processes and practices that impact student success; however, none of that investment will yield the intended results if the performer in each role does not have the talent, capability, and attributes required to be successful in that role and its context. Jim Collins, in his best-selling book, *Good to Great,* emphasized that getting the "right people on the bus" was not sufficient. He pointed to having the right person (an effective performer) in each seat on the bus (or in each job assignment) as critical for achieving the targeted outcomes and results (2001, p. 63).

No doubt during your practice in schools, you will encounter "square pegs in round holes": people who are not well-suited to their assignments. To truly perform as a performance consultant, your practice must support those who hire and assign the adults in the schools in developing and refining their hiring and assignment practices to ensure that each performer is matched to the needs of their job. They may say to you, "We are too small (busy, overwhelmed, etc.) to have a performance and talent management system." The reality is that there *is* a performance and talent management system that is not explicit and has evolved over time. Your role is help those leading the school to recognize the default system that exists and replace it with a system built on best practices for getting, developing, and keeping high-performing team members in the right roles.

This work begins by identifying the common core competencies, or *critical attributes*, needed to be an effective performer in the unique context of the school or district. The *Common Core Competency Guidelines* (Tool 7.1)

Tool 7.1 Common Core Competencies Guidelines

Guidelines: Follow these steps for developing common core competencies:

1. Identify performers in your district or school at every level who have been successful and who have achieved the goals of their school or assignment.

2. What competencies do all those people share?

3. Refine the list to no more than 10 competencies.

4. Widely communicate the list and use it to guide recruiting, selecting, assigning, and developing employees in all jobs and at all levels.

outline an exercise you can use to help those who recruit, hire, assign, develop, and evaluate administrators, teachers, counselors, and other staff.

Using *Common Core Competencies Guidelines*, assemble a cross section of internal and external stakeholders and facilitate them through the process of defining common core competencies, the essential few competencies expected of a job, group, or all employees of the organization. They are *common* in that they are shared, typical, expected, and assumed of employees at all levels in and on behalf of the organization. They are *core* in that they are the essential few (less than 10) competencies required of everyone. Once defined, those attributes can support the development of a workforce well suited to the needs of the students and community the school serves.

As a school improvement specialist, you may be unsure if the work of this standard is within your responsibility, because it focuses on organizational processes and practices that may involve others outside the school, such as central office staff. Because you must look systemically at the factors in the work, workers, and workplace to improve performance, you must do all you can to address those factors by working with those who own the processes and practices that are producing the current results. If you are working in a school within a large district, you may feel that you have no access to those who impact the larger organizational factors or have little influence in changing the processes and practices. You may be right; however, there are some steps you can take at the level of the organization you can impact. The *Hiring and Assigning Guidelines* in Tool 7.2 can be used to troubleshoot the hiring, selection, and assignment process and facilitate providing data and information to those who impact those processes at the school level.

Tool 7.2　　Hiring and Assigning Guidelines

Guidelines: Use the following questions to facilitate a series of meetings with school leaders to derive guidelines that they can use to help them recruit the best talent and assign appropriate tasks to that talent.

1. What does an analysis of available data regarding retirements, transfers, resignations, and dismissals or nonrenewals indicate about the staffing needs for the upcoming hiring period? For the next three to five hiring periods?

2. Which individual jobs most impact the ability to meet the goals or achieve targeted performance improvements? Are each of those assignments staffed with high-performing individuals? If not, what needs to be done to get and keep the right performer into each of those assignments? If it is not possible to hire and assign a high-performer, how else can the need be met?

3. Which other jobs or individual assignments support the ability to meet goals and achieve the desired levels of performance? Are the individuals in each of these roles willing and able to perform at the level of performance needed? If not, what needs to be done to ensure that they are willing and able? If it is not possible to hire and assign willing and able individuals, how else can the need be met?

4. Which roles or assignments do not impact the ability to meet goals and achieve the desired levels of performance? Is the work of the role necessary? If so, what is the best way to get that work done without using resources needed to support more critical roles?

5. Do the job descriptions of each role correctly reflect the work of each job and the current requirements? If not, what revisions are needed? If so, are those job descriptions being used effectively in the recruiting, interviewing, and assigning processes?

6. Does the interview process use prepared behavioral interview questions that inquire into actual examples of an individual's past performance in the actions and decisions that will be expected in the role? What evidence shows that the interview questions used are effective in predicting applicants' on-the-job performance?

As you work with those who hire and assign the adults in the organization to recognize the importance of doing that work well, amid the various constraints of contracts, collective bargaining agreements, and talent pools, your role is to reduce the time spent on people problems and increase the time spent on the work of improving teaching and learning. Just as a new classroom teacher cannot effectively guide learning until classroom management is mastered, those who lead schools cannot be effective at leading improvement until the people problems are addressed. Schools are complex social and political systems within complex school districts and local communities. People problems must be addressed, but how they are addressed will determine the ability of the leader and you as a performance consultant to be effective in your role and to be able to complete your assignment.

Your first question when faced with a people problem should be "*Can this person do what is needed?*" This is a question of capability and, as discussed in earlier chapters, is the litmus test for deciding whether that person needs developmental support. If you have proof of capability, development is not the right intervention.

"Is this person *willing* to do what is needed?" is the next question. If the person is not willing, your role is to explore what is motivating the current performance or demotivating the desired performance and to work with the individual and his or her supervisor to align rewards and consequences of performance. Again, developmental interventions are not appropriate solutions for those who lack the willingness to perform.

"Is this person *able* to do what is needed?" is a question that applies to a person who is judged to be both capable and willing. This question points to the types of factors in the work, workers, and workplace that are impacting performance, particularly those that are beyond the control of the individual performers, which were discussed earlier and require nondevelopmental interventions. One exception, however, is the person who is able to perform but lacks confidence. Coaching is an effective developmental intervention for those judged to be *able* but not *confident*. If the lack of confidence is rooted in fear of the consequences of failure, your role is to work with the performer and his or her supervisor to create an environment in which effort and incremental improvement are rewarded and safe conditions to take risks are provided and protected.

"Does this person *know what is expected?*" is a key question relative to every performer. Before being able to develop people, coach them or evaluate their practice and performance. They deserve to know exactly what is expected of them and how good is good enough. Your role is to work with those who must set and communicate expectations to be clear and precise.

For example, if you ask the supervisor of a principal what is expected of the person in that role, you might hear a response like, "I want that principal to be a strong instructional leader." If you analyze that response, you will see that it includes the label *instructional leader* rather than specific performance expectations. Your role is to ask, "What would I see and hear that person doing on the job that would indicate that he or she is a strong instructional leader?" Probe for specific observable actions and what would be accepted as evidence of the expected results. Help the supervisor record and communicate these expectations.

The following questions can help guide the supervisor to be clear and precise in communicating performance expectations and preparing to assess performance and give feedback:

1. Have you formally communicated the specific observable actions, results, and goals to be met to all the individuals in the job group and to each individual?

2. Are these actions, results, and goals in writing? How long ago was this communicated in writing and reviewed with each individual?

3. Do the expectations match the current job description?

4. Does the performance evaluation, both interim (formative) and summative (overall), match the communicated performance expectations?

When the Gallup organization researched and published the performance factors that impact individuals' engagement and, in turn, their performance and results, it defined a person knowing what is expected of him or her at work as *critical*. Gallup also defined ten other factors, among them, the individual having someone within the last six months talk to him or her about progress toward meeting expectations and recognize or praise him or her for work that has been done well (Gallup, 2010).

In 2004, the Corporate Executive Board published the results of a study of the factors that impact the performance of individuals in their organizations and overall organizational performance. The fairness and accuracy of informal feedback was determined to be the top performance driver (Corporate Leadership Council, 2004). To drive improved performance, feedback must come from a source that is knowledgeable of the individual's on-the-job performance and must give information that helps the person to do the job better.

Good feedback results in increased engagement of the performer and increased, focused effort. In other words, good feedback motivates people to choose to achieve more with their resources, including their time and talents. When coaching performance, you must help those you are guiding to recognize that what they do on the job is a matter of choice, and they are in control of those choices every day.

Your role is to give good informal feedback and train supervisors to do the same. Good informal feedback meets the following criteria:

- It is frequent.
- It separates the person from the performance.
- It is specific.
- It focuses on observable performance (what was done or not done).
- It identifies the resulting personal, organizational, and student impacts and consequences.
- It includes specific suggestions, developed with the performer, of how to do the job better.
- It identifies and builds on strengths.

Gallup and the Conference Board found that people who are allowed to apply their strengths to their work are more engaged and effective and their organizations are more successful. By determining and communicating the strengths of those you are facilitating, you are able to better align their assignments and contributions to the goals. You want your feedback to emphasize strengths as well as opportunities and needs for development and improved performance. As you model this analysis and feedback process for leaders, you will support them in adopting these practices within their school.

Gallup and the Conference Board also found that emphasis on strengths during formal performance evaluations was critical to keeping performers engaged so that they could make needed changes in their behavior and on-the-job performance. A summative evaluation can be an anxiety-producing event for both the evaluator and the performer. A strengths-based approach can set the tone for a positive, helpful assessment discussion that is focused upon helping the performer. The feedback during formal or summative evaluations will never be a surprise for those assessed if informal feedback has been frequent, accurate, and specific. Good informal feedback also helps to reduce the anxiety on the part of both the performer and the evaluator when conducting formal evaluations.

If you and the supervisors you are facilitating through the improvement process do a good job of providing informal daily feedback, you are likely to find that the performer may be more critical of his or her own performance than you, a supervisor, or peers. When adults are kept informed enough to clearly see the gap between what they are doing and could be doing, they are much less likely to be resistant to performance feedback and evaluation.

Good interim or formative performance evaluations are not solely about judgment of performance. They are also focused on reviewing and communicating expectations, finding solutions to problems, and providing needed resources, including information, time, tools, and technology. They are about breaking the work ahead down into manageable steps aligned with long-term goals and targeted results. Good interim evaluations focus on multiple measures of performance, including progress and adoption indicators. Adoption indicators are set with the performer and identify the types of evidence the performer will provide along the way to monitor implementation of initiatives and projects and to determine if the work is progressing as intended and will achieve the intended results.

Formal evaluations assess the aggregated data and performance evidence against the preset performance expectations and criteria. Again, multiple measures of performance support systemic improvement are needed to avoid a focus on, or the manipulation of, individual or single performance metric to the detriment of other types of performance and results. Evaluations, both interim and summative, are legal documents, and care must be taken to ensure that they are valid, fair, and legally defensible.

If performance evaluations are being administered correctly, you can study completed assessments to determine gaps in individuals' and groups' performances that are impeding reaching targeted results, and you can then align performance interventions based on that data. If your study reveals that most or all individuals are meeting standards but the organization is not meeting its goals or performance targets, supervisors will need support in learning to develop good performance feedback and to appropriately use evaluations as performance interventions for teachers, administrators, and staff.

Building capacity is the central role of facilitators of school improvement; however, if the focus is mainly on developing capability and does not include interventions to improve hiring, selection, assignment, and evaluation, then the gains made are not likely to be sustainable. If developmental interventions are not developed using best practices in adult learning and performance support, they will not be as effective as they could be. You must build your own capacity to be a good model for performance and talent management in order to transfer those skills into practice by those who will lead the organization in the future.

AN EXAMPLE OF AN EFFECTIVE APPLICATION OF STANDARD 7

Smythe Porter was hired as a consultant to support a school district that had expanded its accountability system to focus upon multiple measures of student, administrator, teacher, and staff performance and to complete the development of a five-year strategic plan with emphasis on excellence, equity, and engagement. Porter was assigned by the superintendent to work with each school to align its school improvement plan to the strategic plan and was provided a draft of the new strategic plan, current performance data, and information the district office and school leadership teams had collected from several internal and community stakeholder input sessions. The superintendent said to Porter, "I think we have a good draft strategic plan and the right performance indicators. I need you to tell us what, if anything, we have overlooked."

Over the next week, Porter reviewed the draft strategic plan, performance data, school improvement plans, and inquiry sessions with the key owners of the related action plans and with those who worked for the district in a variety of positions. He scheduled time to present the findings to the superintendent, district staff, and the school leadership teams. He presented his findings and recommendations for each of the four primary goal areas of the strategic plan: (1) *Student Achievement;* (2) *Organizational Effectiveness;* (3) *Student, Staff, and Stakeholder Engagement;* and (4) *Team Learning, Growth, and Performance.*

When he reached the point in the presentation for reviewing the fourth goal, he issued a challenge to the group. "I believe you have significant work ahead to improve the interventions and practices associated with Goal Area 4: *Team Learning, Growth, and Performance.* You need to adopt and implement a systemic and purposeful talent and performance management system that addresses each of the critical subsystems listed here."

Porter pointed to the list that represented the elements of an aligned performance and talent management continuum, with each rated against a scale of (1) Needs to Be Developed, (2) Developing, (3) Effective, or (4) Highly Effective. The results were as follows:

- Forecasting Talent Needs: 1
- Recruitment: 2

- Hiring and Selection: 2
- Assignment: 2
- Entry Induction Process by Job Type: 2
- Role Transition Inductions: 1
- Development: 3
- Feedback and Formative Assessment: 1
- Feedback and Summative Assessment: 2
- Correcting Underperformance: 2
- Motivating Peak Performance: 2
- Performance and Talent Management Alignment: 1

Porter then presented the evidence that supported the rating of each element, allowing time for discussion of each element and rating. At the conclusion of the rating discussion, he asked the group, "Based on what we have just reviewed, what do you recognize that needs to be done to establish an aligned performance and talent management system that is tailored to your local contexts, strengths, needs, and challenges?"

Porter facilitated the development of a list of action items related to each element and promised to return to the group with a plan for closing the gap between current practices and those the group identified were needed. The group provided input on who to engage in planning teams to define the steps and tasks that they must lead, participate in implementing, or supervise.

About four weeks later, Porter proposed new objectives for Goal Area 4 on the strategic plan and facilitated the planning teams in presenting action plans that were aligned to each element and aligned with the new objectives on the strategic plan. After each plan was reviewed, adjusted, and approved, Porter worked with the teams for the next two weeks to lay out a timeline with progress checks and adoption indicators. The teams presented their work plans and gained approval to complete a systemic set of interventions over the coming year. One team, who called themselves *The Talent Scouts*, presented plans for forecasting talent needs, developing common core competencies, updating job descriptions, and revising interview protocols to include behavioral interviews, team interviews, and portfolio reviews. Another team, *The Induction Function*, presented plans for supporting new hires into the organization and a process called "Catch a Rising Star" to support performers who were transitioning into new roles and responsibilities or who needed to achieve readiness for new roles. A third team, *Know-How,* had researched best practices for developing adults in schools and had developed a comprehensive process for determining when development was needed, for whom, and which guidelines were the most efficient and effective for building capacity. The final team, *CSI* (or *Competent School Investigators*), presented their research on formative and summative evaluations, use of performance portfolios in evaluation, and a process for implementing new evaluation instruments and practices over the next three years by working with a recognized local expert in fair, valid, and legal appraisal and with an expert in assessment for learning. The group recommended a series of training programs for supervisors in providing performance feedback and conducting performance appraisals.

As the planning teams converted themselves into implementation teams, Porter worked with the teams, supervisors, and others responsible for the districts' performance and talent management system to develop their planned interventions and align them into what they came to refer to as their districts' *Signature Performance and Talent Management System.*

Early in the second year of support of the work of Goal 4, Porter met with the superintendent. "Your teams have made good progress on the Signature Performance and Talent Management System. Because you have actively monitored the implementation of your interventions, every element of the system is rating at a level 3 (*Effective*), except *Recruitment.* Due to effectiveness in all the other elements and a deep pool of applicants, recruitment has not seemed to be an urgent focus. The next steps are to better forecast the skills that students need to master for college and career readiness in jobs that may not even exist today and to recruit or even contract with individuals who can support mastery in those skills. That focus and analysis should help reach effectiveness in the recruitment element. My assignment here is drawing to a close, and I want to both thank you for your leadership of the interventions and your support for me as your performance consultant. Your team has adopted new processes into their practices, and with continued oversight, you should continue to see related gains in student performance as adult performance continues to improve."

AN EXAMPLE OF A LESS EFFECTIVE APPLICATION OF STANDARD 7

Estella Brooker was assigned to facilitate the improvement of a school that was struggling to meet the requirements of a new accountability system. After conducting a review of the school's performance data against a new, expanded set of performance measures, Estella led teams of administrators, teachers, and staff through analysis of the causes of underperformance rooted in curriculum, assessment, instruction, professional development, and technology. She helped the teams to update the school improvement plan and to develop new action plans to address the causes identified. The teams identified a suite of interventions including learning communities; classroom walk-throughs; short, focused observation of teaching compared to specific standards; adoption of standards-based grading processes; and professional learning on scheduled workdays to support improved differentiation of instruction.

After six months of facilitating improvement efforts in the school, she presented her plans and progress to the state coordinator who supervised her assignment. "You have done an excellent job of supporting adoption of teaching and learning improvements at the classroom level. What evidence do you have that the capacity of those who work in the school will be sufficient by the end of the year to sustain progress without your involvement in the school? Does the school have the talent it needs to successfully become a high-performing school? What system of monitoring and managing performance will the administrators and district staff use to ensure fidelity of implementation beyond your assignment?"

REFLECTION

1. What did Porter do to help to build capacity of adults?

2. What else does Brooker need to do to ensure long-term sustainability of the work she began?

3. What in this chapter will be useful to you as you build capacity in the schools you serve?

POWER POINTS

Here are some suggestions about how to do this work:

- Take the time to learn about adult learning theory and project-based instructional methods. Share what you learn with the teachers and leaders you are supporting.

- Practice asking yourself reflective questions, especially if you feel overwhelmed or frustrated over the amount of work to be done. Being reflective yourself will help you model the behaviors you want to see in others as well as advance your own level of proficiency.
- Create a learning community for yourself. Use that community to help you learn best practices as well as receive support, guidance, and reassurance.

SUMMARY

This chapter has been about transferring the capability of doing school improvement work to others. Transferring capability is an essential component of sustaining gains in student, teacher, and leader performance. Developing others' capability to do the complex work of school improvement also requires you to set aside your own ego and trust others to develop their own methods and style. You want to provide a sufficient level of guidance so others experience success early and therefore become confident in their ability to do this work. At the same time, you have to provide backup in case they slip or struggle at certain points. The ultimate indicator of your success as a facilitator of school improvement work is others' ability to do the work in your absence.

See the end of this book for a complete list of resources and references related to building capacity.

Additional materials and resources related to
The School Improvement Specialist Field Guide
can be found on the companion website.
http://www.corwin.com/sisguide

Demonstrate Organizational Sensitivity

8

"I never thought you would be asking me for fashion advice," Frank Perez said as he teased Bailey Pittman. "As I recall, you were always the well-dressed one when we were in class together at the university."

"It's not exactly a fashion issue," Bailey laughed. "I am trying to decide when to wear a suit to work and when I should dress more casually. I don't want to be intimidating, but I want to reflect professionalism. As a principal, I always wore a suit or dress, usually something with a jacket. The teachers in the school dress in what they call professional casual, which usually is slacks and a collared shirt for men and pants or a skirt and top or a dress for women. What is the rule of thumb for consultants in a situation like this?"

"Generally it is advisable to dress at a level that is equal or slightly better than those you are guiding. For example, I usually do not wear a suit when doing teacher observations, since the teachers here do not wear suits or ties. I will wear a tie and jacket for meetings that include administrators or external stakeholders or for a board meeting. I try to determine the norms of the school for adults' attire and always look neat and conservative," Frank explained.

"I had a talk yesterday with one of the principals in the school I am helping," Bailey told Frank. "He said he had always worn a tie to school, but he came to suspect that some of the parents were uneasy coming into the school because they did not have business attire to wear. He told me he purposefully chose not to wear a tie when having parent meetings, so he could better relate to them. After I had that conversation, I began to wonder if I should or should not wear a suit every day."

"Every school has its norms, explicit or implicit, about how people dress, relate, and engage each other. You have to observe and identify their norms and take your cues from them. Sometimes you have to help those you are leading to revisit their norms and establish norms that are more aligned to the results they are seeking. From our past discussions, it seems that you have been successful in getting others to relate to you and that you have done a great deal of listening and observing and are able to influence others," Frank observed.

159

"Our role as improvement specialists," he continued, "requires that we keep an eye on the processes that impact teaching and learning and guide others to improve those processes and practices. We also have to pay close attention to the people issues if we want to achieve the type of changes the school needs. I have spent a great deal of time coaching the administrators, staff, and teacher leaders about how they relate to the faculty, students, families, and stakeholders. I tell them that every interaction they have is a chance to make a deposit or withdrawal in what I call their 'trust and respect account.' If their actions, decisions, and communication encourage and honor others and increase trust, credibility, and mutual respect, they are much more likely to be able to get those they are leading to act in a manner that contributes to meeting the schools' goals."

"It is amazing that much of what influences people is not what is said but who says it, how it is said, and what people conclude from what they observe," Bailey concluded. "Every day, I feel like I peel back another layer of the onion and get a better understanding of what causes the school and those in it to perform as they do."

To be continued . . .

STANDARD 8: DEMONSTRATE ORGANIZATIONAL SENSITIVITY

Collectively, the elements of Standard 8 clarify the roles and behaviors that distinguish successful diplomats and leaders from those who are not as successful; many of these roles and behaviors are required to effectively facilitate people through the school improvement process. Figure 8.1 illustrates how the consulting process must be done in conjunction with the performance improvement process. Effective consultants know the importance of following the performance improvement process while staying attentive to the people whose engagement and cooperation are essential to success. The performances described in this chapter take a closer look at the behaviors that underlie the consulting side of the work of school improvement.

Figure 8.1   Parallel Processes

Performance Improvement Process	
1. Performance Analysis	One eye on the goal
2. Cause Analysis	
3. Intervention Design and Development	
4. Intervention Implementation and Evaluation	
Consultative Process	
1. Advise, Confront, and Give Feedback	One eye on the people
2. Model Behaviors and Coach	
3. Facilitate Discovery and Decision Making	
4. Maneuver the Political Landscape	

When done well, completing both of these processes will allow you to influence people's decisions. When done poorly, you will be considered an outcast and your ideas and information will either be discounted or distorted, so people can justify their unwillingness to cooperate with you to bring about positive change.

Establishing Credibility

The first element of Standard 8 is about building and protecting your reputation. It is about how to be seen as a credible person, so your ideas are given a fair hearing.

8.1 Establish professional credibility, gain respect, and build trust.

Credibility is the product of trust and respect. When you are first assigned the role of school improvement specialist, people may afford you some initial courtesies, but this is not the same as respecting your expertise or trusting your intentions.

Credibility is the product of trust and respect.

Typically what people do is listen to your words and watch your actions. They are searching for evidence that you

- have some comprehension of and appreciation for the complexity of their unique situation.
- will respect them and their ideas.
- will genuinely listen to their ideas and positions.
- are consistent in your responses and positions while also being open to change, based on a fair consideration of their ideas.
- keep your word.
- do not use their words or ideas to discount them.
- maintain confidences.
- have the support and confidence of the other school leaders.

The challenge for you is finding out what people will accept as evidence you are credible, trustworthy, and worthy of their respect. The answer is a combination of what you do (your behavior), how you look (your appearance), what you say (your knowledge and expertise), how you sound when you say it (your words and language), to whom you speak or not (your inclusiveness), and what you put in writing (your writing clarity). On the surface, these appear to be easily accomplished behaviors; however, in practice they are not that easy.

Allison Edy, a school improvement specialist, has what she calls a *trust meter* that she uses to find out who among the group is respected for his or her expertise, who is trusted for his or her integrity, and who can be relied on for accurate information. She uses the technique not to judge her own level of credibility but to help her further earn the trust of the group. Edy asks everyone in the group individually three questions either during casual conversations or during prearranged sessions set up for another reason. She records their responses on a chart (see the *Trust Meter Chart* in Tool 8.1). The questions are intended to find out who they consider credible, who they consider trustworthy, and who they like. The answers may or may not point to the same person. Here are some of the questions Edy asks:

Trust and respect (This requires *admitting* a lack of expertise and a need for help; people tend to do this with people they trust and whose opinion they regard.)

1. Who do you go to when you are having a problem in the classroom and want some guidance on what to do? *or* Who do you go to when you want some help or feedback about how things are working?

Credibility (This requires *declaring* whose opinion or information they consider to be valid.)

2. Who do you rely on when you want to find out what's really going on? *or* When you hear a rumor, to whom do you go to find out the truth?

Liking (This requires *revealing* with whom they are comfortable.)

3. Who do you usually hang out with when the school sponsors an event like a race or picnic? *or* Is there anyone in particular you prefer to get together with on a social basis?

Edy uses the results of her questions to find out who among the group are the informal leaders, who have the greatest influence on the group, and who are the most accessible. These are the same people whose trust and respect she must earn. She then looks for patterns in responses that may indicate subgroups. Finally, she looks for the people whose names were never or rarely mentioned, as they may be the outliers, the newcomers, or the ones others distrust. She must honor their perspectives as well. When doing this, she must be especially careful to not betray confidences and to not be seen as taking sides. She must take extra steps to be inclusive and solicit the opinions of everyone.

Tool 8.1   Trust Meter Chart

Guidelines: Follow the steps below to get an understanding of who the group deems as credible.

Plan.

- Decide what you want to find out. For example, do you want to identify potential leaders, possible experts, or find out how the group members relate to each other?
- Develop two to three questions that will ask group members to choose other members of the group.

Ask each group member the questions. Let people know that their responses will be confidential.

Compile the responses in a table, placing the names of those you questioned in Column 1 and the names of the people they chose in Column 2.

Tally the number of times each person was chosen by counting the number of times their name appears in Column 2 and put the total in Column 3, titled *Times Chosen*.

Review the chart and note the following:

- those chosen most often
- those never chosen
- pairs who chose each other
- pairs or small groups that are not chosen by anyone outside their pair or small group. They appear as separate from the larger group.

Note the number of individuals that exchange information (chose each other) or just give or receive information (the choosing was not reciprocal).

Formulate some hypotheses as to why the pattern is as it seems.

Consider other data or pursue other data collection methods to confirm or disprove your hypotheses.

First Question			
Column 1:	Column 2:	Column 3: Times Chosen	Comments
Group Members	Who They Chose		

Following Accepted Rules

The second element of Standard 8 is about honoring the social norms of the group.

> 8.2 Follow accepted rules of etiquette, precedence, or conventions appropriate to the context.

Groups establish norms to help them survive in the world. Sometimes those norms promote harmony, and sometimes they prevent progress. Families and how they operate best illustrate the concept of group norms. For example, one family agrees that despite the host's request to not bring anything to dinner, you should always come with a bottle of wine, a side dish, or a dessert. In a different family, you would not do this, as it would be seen as an insult to the host. Members of a third family know to offer guests a beverage three times, because the guest knows it is proper to accept only on the third offering. To not extend the offer three times or to accept an earlier offer would be considered rude. A different family might extend the offer once and never bring it up again, and this would be considered appropriate. One family knows that "dinner at six" really means you show up at 6:30. Another family knows to show up between 5:00 and 5:15 for social pleasantries and that dinner will be served right at 6:00.

School systems also operate on an agreed-on set of norms. However, they present themselves differently. For example, in one school, everyone waits until the unofficial group leader speaks first. One group may have decided that it is okay to voice dissenting opinions. Another group has agreed that differences are to be discussed behind closed doors, not in an open arena. Yet another group considers debate a sign of health and encourages opposing opinions. Groups also decide who is allowed latitude when it comes to certain rules, like not getting materials in on time. It is important to discuss, clarify, and agree on the group's norms. Over time, precedents are set about who gets invited to work sessions, how invitations are communicated, who gets invited first, whose time is compensated, when meetings are held, and more. To learn about group norms and precedents, observe and ask.

For example, John Barkley has been successful at helping turn around schools for more than five years. A technique he learned from his mentor was to do a cultural audit early in the assignment. He usually begins the process when doing the initial data gathering (see the *Initial Inquiry Worksheet* (Tool 1.2) and *Assumptions Worksheet* (Tool 1.4) in Chapter 1). In addition to capturing responses from the group when doing the initial analysis of the school, he pays attention to:

- who arranges for the meeting space.
- how invitations are sent out and who does it.
- who comes early to set up the space, if that is required.
- who speaks first in the meeting once the work is underway.
- who adds to or builds on the information already presented.
- who confirms the information already presented with phrases like "That's right."
- who and how many rarely, if ever, come forth with a response.
- who and how many offer dissenting information or interpretations.
- who sits where and who sits with whom.

He uses this information to begin to formulate hypotheses about the openness and inclusiveness of the group, its norms, and its communication protocols. He then further uses his observations to help him demonstrate respect for the group's way of operating before he begins to offer suggestions on how to operate differently. He learned over time that people are more apt to change if they first feel their perspectives were honored. John uses an *Interaction Worksheet* (shown in Tool 8.2) to study the exchanges and communication of the group.

Tool 8.2   Interaction Worksheet

Guidelines:

1. Decide what behaviors you want to track or count the frequency of when observing people in a group setting.

2. Identify the person or people you want to observe.

3. Create a worksheet to record when the behaviors occur. Figure 8.2 is an example of possible behaviors to observe.

4. Put the initials of the people you want to observe in the first row.

5. List the types of behaviors you want to track in the first column.

6. Explain the purpose of the observation and what information will be shared with them when it is over.

7. Discuss how you will handle exceptions like confidential exchanges.

(Continued)

(Continued)

8. To record their patterns of interactions, you can use a check-mark. You can continue the chart when the subject changes.

Interaction Worksheet										
Initials										
behaviors	1	2	3	4	5	6	7	8	9	10

The *Interaction Worksheet* uses a process that is a modified version of the *Flanders Interaction Analysis,* developed by Ned Flanders to study teachers' interactions with students (Flanders, 1970). The results can be used to determine the type of verbal and nonverbal communication people engage in, such as order giving, answering, active listening, passive listening, social interaction, and so on. This information can measure interpersonal skills of people who are expected to coach or lead teams. This process was designed to help observers be more disciplined and consistent in their observations of group behavior. You can adapt the process to help you be more cognizant of how groups communicate among themselves and with outsiders.

Figure 8.2   Example of an Interaction Worksheet

Initials	Interaction Worksheet															
	1	2	3	4	5	6	7	8	9	10	11	12	13	14	15	16
Give advice																
Pass judgment																
Paraphrase																
Clarify																
Acknowledge																
Give credit																
Other																

Demonstrating Professionalism

The third element of Standard 8 is about a person's observable behavior and demeanor and how that influences people's judgment and decisions.

> 8.3 Demonstrate a high level of professionalism through appropriate dress, speech, written communication, and behavior.

Professionalism, like beauty, is in the eye of the beholder; therefore, this element is about others' reactions to your personal appearance and communication practices, both verbal and written. The important rule to remember is to keep the focus on the goal (that phase of the project you are in) and not on you. Owning a beautiful piece of jewelry is rewarding in itself, but it may not be appropriate to wear it if it distracts people's attention or fosters questions about you, how much money you make, or your taste in jewelry rather than the subject under discussion. People judge you based on your haircut, the condition of your shoes, the length of your dress or skirt, the tightness or looseness of your shirt or pants, and the overall condition of your apparel. Appearing too stylish may create barriers, especially when working with schools in economically disadvantaged areas. At the same time, looking just like everyone else may also create barriers, as they want you to bring a new perspective.

Keep the focus on the goal, not on you.

Conceptually, you want to exhibit enough of the group's norms to be accepted but be different enough to suggest you will bring fresh ideas and leadership. People are prone to judge your maturity based on your attire and hairstyle. You do not want to be seen as emulating a new Hollywood star or competing with the other members of the team. Unfortunately, if you are too different, you risk being seen as an outcast, someone to be distrusted. Every group has norms, and it is important to honor those. However, a group's leader has to be a little out of the norm, otherwise there are no new behaviors to emulate that will result in change or improvement. A group leader must walk the fine line between being seen as part of the group and being different enough to warrant respect, all while not being so different as to become estranged from the group. Figure 8.3 illustrates the difference between a leader or influencer and a group outlier.

Figure 8.3   Influencers and Outliers

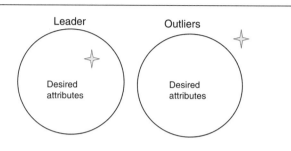

The challenge is to identify the attributes held by most members of the group. You can also use this concept when coaching members of the team to assume a larger leadership role.

In addition to purposefully capturing a group's communication patterns, John Barkley, a school improvement specialist who purposefully analyzes interactions of group members when he is working to influence change and improvement, also works to identify the attributes and values that are held in esteem by the group. He starts by finding out where members of the group went to school, what their degrees are in, how many served in the military or currently have family serving, how many leaders and administrators have classroom experience and at what level, how many have family employed by the school system and other employers in the community, how many grew up in the community, how many have family attending the school system, how many attend religious institutions and which ones, and so on. He is sensitive to personal friendships and professional loyalties and interdependencies (such as who has family members also employed by the school or school district). He does not try to replicate these factors but uses them in his conversations and in helping him decide who to approach and how.

Next, he looks for patterns in behavior, dress, activities that may indicate which attributes the group tries to emulate or avoid. Typically, leaders hire people like themselves—that is, they tend to hire people with the same outlook on life, hobbies, background, and so on. When done to the extreme, the group is more prone to *group think* and may find it harder to challenge their assumptions about students, teachers, and leaders. John uses this insight to help him formulate ways to engage everyone. He also uses it to help him decide on what to wear when meeting people in either formal or informal settings.

People will also judge you on your written communication and speaking style. It is very important that you take the time to check your spelling, grammar, and syntax. Your e-mail and written messages have to be logical and clear. When speaking, you do not need to be eloquent, but you do need to be clear, monitor your grammar, be selective in your use of local jargon, and keep your style somewhat formal. People tend to draw conclusions based on your writing and speaking styles, and based on what they read or hear, they may conclude you are careless, not respectful, or incompetent. The best way to avoid negative conclusions is to take the time to construct your messages carefully; ideally, you should ask someone to read important communications before sending them out.

John Green, a high-performing high school principal who recently became superintendent in Jackson County Schools, is a master communicator and influencer. He uses a modified Information Mapping™ style in all of his written communications. His style is to point out the purpose of the message, what he expects from the reader (understanding, a decision, agreement, or a change of behavior). He is careful to stick to the point. Some of the conventions he has developed include the following:

1. Clearly state the purpose of the message.

2. Point out when an action or decision is required.

3. Note what the expected response time is.

4. Clarify the intent when presenting data or information.

5. Point out the source of data.

6. Either solicit comments about possible interpretations of data or suggest possible meanings.

7. Ask for time for discussion.

8. Indicate when a follow up will occur.

9. Take the time to check spelling and grammar.

10. Resist the temptation of adding on a new topic.

In addition to your appearance, people judge you on how you sound. Your speech does not have to sound like the local dialect. It is more important that you pronounce your words correctly, avoid errors in verb tense, and be organized. You may find it helpful to have yourself audio or video recorded and then listen to or watch yourself.

Valuing Others' Positions and Views

The fourth element of Standard 8 is about your behavior and interactions with others.

8.4 Interact in ways that make people feel their roles, positions, and views are valued.

The words of significance in this element are "people feel..." The group you are working with will watch you. They will look for inconsistencies in your behavior, perhaps to justify an initial decision to not fully engage or to dismiss you and your work as intrusive. You are not *one of them,* but an expert in facilitating school improvement. However, as an expert, your role is not to judge or dictate but to engage by soliciting information and giving evidence that you heard what others said. This performance is less about you actually hearing what people say and more about people feeling you heard and understood them. People draw conclusions about whether or not you heard them by what you say and what you do afterwards.

One of the challenges is that people are not always proficient in expressing what they know, what they believe to be true, how they feel about the situation, or on what basis they are drawing their conclusions. Therefore, your job is to hear the intent behind the message, not just the words that are used. The real message may be in what is not overtly discussed; it may be in a group's behaviors, such as letting one person speak for them instead of taking responsibility for sharing their own opinions. The real message may be hidden due to self-censorship, when people withhold information, because they believe it will be discounted. Whatever the reason that people share or choose not to share, they are paying attention to your reactions. Some will be hoping you can hear beyond the words, can pick up on what is not overtly said, and can read between the lines. To do this will require you to purposefully and repeatedly solicit everyone's opinion, to confirm your understanding, and to ask for help when messages seem to be unclear or contradictory. You do not have to do all of the work yourself. Listening and reacting are opportunities to engage.

Edy, like Green, pays attention to who speaks and how often as well as what is said and not said. One of the techniques she uses is to confirm the intent behind the message, and she asks others to help her understand. She uses phrases like "If I heard you correctly, you said [she paraphrases what was said], and I think I heard you say [she adds her interpretation or embellishment], and the reason you are telling me this is you want me to [she shares what she thinks is the expected reaction]. Is this accurate [she asks for confirmation]?" If another person witnessed the exchange, Edy may engage that person by asking, "You heard what was said; did I get the meaning correct?" Edy goes beyond paraphrasing and makes it a practice to state what she believes is the purpose or intent of the message. By doing this, she fosters engagement and self-responsibility for the accuracy of the message.

Keeping People Engaged

The final element for Standard 8 is about acting in ways that keep people engaged long enough to adopt and commit to new behaviors, whether that be teaching, leading, or supporting each other differently.

> 8.5 Behave in ways that increase the likelihood that people stay engaged and honor their commitments.

This is about your being consistent in your behaviors and appearance and making sure you do not inadvertently create barriers that deter people from sharing or taking responsibility for what is or is not happening. This is the perhaps the most challenging of the five elements for this standard, as it is about being consistent.

Green and Edy make time in their schedules to reflect, rest, and recharge. They have learned that when they are tired or try to respond to too many people at once, they are more apt to be curt, say something inappropriate, misinterpret someone's behavior or words, or overlook an opportunity to further engage and reinforce new behaviors. They remind themselves of how important it is to think in the long term while being purposively attentive to the people whose commitment they require to accomplish the goals they have set.

AN EXAMPLE OF AN EFFECTIVE APPLICATION OF STANDARD 8

Superintendent Paula Veal thanked Vince Cameron, president of School Transformation Initiatives, for the efforts of his team over the past two years in working with her school district to increase the graduation rate, college and career readiness rate, and the progression of students from year-to-year using a small-schools-within-schools model. "Your three consultants brought valuable expertise to the district, and the data shows the middle school and high school transformation program is getting the results it is intended to achieve. The faculty, staff, and community were initially skeptical that the widespread changes were for the best, but your team has been highly effective in both guiding the changes and bringing everyone along."

"It has been our pleasure," Cameron told her, "and as we make the transition to the last year of our support here, we would like some specific feedback on each of the consultants who worked with you, so we can make any needed adjustments for the final year of the project, based on your needs and preferences."

Superintendent Veal produced a notebook and flipped through several pages of notes, reviewing them with Cameron. "Wendy Booth has been a very strong facilitator at the high school. She is rather quiet and unassuming, but when she speaks, people listen. She gained the trust and respect of everyone at the school by how she listened to them, took their points of view into consideration, and engaged them in making the changes. As she coached the teachers and the rest of the school team, she was very shrewd in how she facilitated those sessions and helped everyone to use the research she provided and their daily experiences to reach their own conclusions that the changes were needed. She is an excellent communicator and has always made people feel valued. In one of the early sessions, a teacher who is very influential with her peers was highly resistant and kept subtly sniping at Wendy during meetings. One day, Wendy calmly turned to her and said, 'That sounded like you were taking a jab at me; did you mean for it to sound that way?' The person stammered that she did not mean to (although it was clear that she had), and Wendy smoothed the situation over by saying how much she respected her opinion and input. Everyone in the group saw that Wendy was not mean-spirited and genuinely wanted to help them. From then on, the tension disappeared and the group was able to move forward on the project together."

"I am glad to hear that. What is your feedback on Scott Dowdy?" Cameron asked.

The superintendent flipped through a few more pages and said, "Scott is also very skilled and practical in working with our middle school transformation. What I have noticed about Scott is that he is very different from Wendy in how he works with people, but equally effective. His dry humor and his optimism is infectious, and even though he does not accept excuses for failure to do what needs to be done for our students, people like and respect him. He is a master communicator, highly professional, and very energetic and engaging. The team at the middle school calls him 'Colonel Dowdy,' but they really respect and admire him. You can be very proud of the work Wendy and Scott have done here. This has been a very different experience than our last consultant engagement. Thank you for sending us such experienced and savvy facilitators. They not only knew how to make the technical changes, but they also were skilled in bringing people along."

AN EXAMPLE OF A LESS EFFECTIVE APPLICATION OF STANDARD 8

Superintendent Veal closed her notebook and smiled at Cameron. "Believe me, it is refreshing to have such capable people working with our team. We had a disaster a few years back, when we hired a consultant who had been an effective superintendent in another district to help us with coaching our principals. It was amazing that someone who had been so effective in her own district was unable to connect with the principals here. She had an answer and advice for every issue and seemed not to understand that she was an outsider to this district and needed to earn everyone's respect and trust before she ordered people around. She was so pushy that some of our principals just shut down and did the minimum needed to work with her. I didn't realize until I did some informal feedback sessions with the principals that the arrangement was not working. I realized my time was better spent coaching the principals and connecting them in peer-to-peer networks than using someone from outside. I felt awkward cancelling her contract with us, because I know she was a very good superintendent. She just had trouble transitioning from being the leader to being a coach and consultant."

REFLECTION

1. What did Scott and Wendy do (even though their styles were different) that made them effective in facilitating transformation in their assigned schools?

2. What did the former superintendent do or fail to do that made her less effective as a performance coach and consultant than she was in her previous role?

3. What in this chapter and in your past experiences will be useful to you when coaching and consulting with others to transform and improve their school(s)?

POWER POINTS

What follows are tips related to becoming more astute when it comes to organizational sensitivity.

- Occasionally read the column called *Miss Manners* that appears in local newspapers. The situations described frequently capture the subtleties of human behavior and the conclusions people draw based on what others do or not do.

- If the opportunity arises, take a course on group communication. It is usually part of the curriculum in a department of communication or behavior sciences. Learning more about group dynamics is a lifelong pursuit. Critical Friends Groups training by the School Reform Initiative can be helpful in facilitating groups. Courses in mediation, conflict resolution, or dealing with difficult people can also be very valuable. Many of these are available online as digital books or through public workshops. Crucial Conversation workshops, books, and tools are widely used to build skills in relating to others, especially in high-stakes situations.

- When doing this work, commit time to care for yourself. Surround yourself with people who will help you rest, reflect, and restore. If you allow yourself to become burned out or overworked, you will be less effective and more prone to making mistakes or missing opportunities.

- Try never to put people in a position where they must choose between change and a friendship. Friendships usually win, even when people know it is not in the best interest of the future.

SUMMARY

This chapter has been about the subtle social and communication skills required to earn others' respect and cooperation. Demonstrating organizational sensitivity is much more than just obeying social norms. It is about respecting people, not prematurely judging people, and delighting in divergent ways people have come to work together. It requires selflessness and a willingness to suppress your own needs for recognition and validation in exchange for celebrating others' individuality and contributions. The tools described in this chapter are based on processes used by social scientists to describe and interpret group norms and identify behaviors that facilitate learning and growth.

See the end of the book for a complete list of resources and references related to organizational sensitivity.

Additional materials and resources related to
The School Improvement Specialist Field Guide
can be found on the companion website.
http://www.corwin.com/sisguide

Monitor Accountability and Adoption

9

"Did you get the invitation I sent you?" Frank Perez asked Bailey Pittman. "We are having a special board presentation of the work we have completed over the last year on a student attendance initiative I have helped to facilitate. I would like you to come to see how we use these presentations to keep our work on track and celebrate our progress."

"Yes, thank you for thinking of me. I plan to attend," Bailey replied. "How did the attendance initiative get started?"

"A couple of years ago, we implemented and cascaded Balanced Scorecards, a performance dashboard, and data rooms at the district level and in each school. Our school boardroom is also a data room. We did this so that when we are making decisions, we are always data driven. As we became more focused on performance data, our administrators, school leadership teams, and improvement teams began to meet regularly to report on progress against the goals and the performance targets we have set. They record, present, and celebrate their achievements and those of their students. Once a quarter, they present to the school board. During one of those sessions, one of the board members pointed to our student attendance performance measures. She noted that student absences averaged more than ten days per year, excluding long-term student illnesses. The board discussed this and charged the district to find ways to reduce the absences by at least 50 percent by the end of the next school year."

"We developed a problem statement and developed a logic chain for it," Frank said. "That is a simple useful tool I will share with you. To make a long story short, we implemented the initiatives you will see showcased at the upcoming meeting, and we established performance measures and adoption indicators, which are the changes and evidence we focused on to determine if we were doing the right work and making progress. We celebrated when we made progress, and when our check-ups showed problems, we addressed them.

"The community responded and addressed factors outside of the school's control. We reduced student absenteeism 60 percent," Frank concluded. "I think you will be impressed."

"I know I will be," Bailey said. "I also want to learn more about how you monitored and held people accountable. I need to focus on that in my current assignment."

To be continued . . .

STANDARD 9: MONITOR ACCOUNTABILITY AND ADOPTION

After all the analysis, planning, and effort to develop others' capacity, your role is to put processes in place that create the discipline required for monitoring, following through, and following up to ensure the selected interventions are implemented with fidelity and achieve the intended outcomes and results. You, no doubt, have witnessed programs that were begun with strong focus and good intentions but were subsequently derailed, abandoned, or implemented in ways that caused the quality of the work to degrade over time. The keys to sustainability are paying attention and keeping attention focused on the work and results. Monitoring and continuous collection of data and information can keep the work on track even after you are no longer guiding the work.

Paying Attention Purposely

The first element of Standard 9 is about the importance of paying attention to the right things.

> 9.1 Check purposefully (keep an eye on) on performance, conditions, and results by observing people's behavior and interim results.

As a school improvement facilitator, you focus on building improvement and project plans for the processes that support teaching, learning, and educator and student success. You guide others not only to carry out the projects and improve processes to achieve specific goals but also to sustain the work after you are no longer supporting their efforts. If you can help those accountable for the results to adopt tools and processes to monitor the interventions, you will significantly increase the likelihood of those solutions being implemented with fidelity and achieving the targeted outcomes.

To help those you are supporting to reach their desired results, you must help them to establish and monitor *performance targets*. Performance targets are the specific desired results expressed as measures. Performance targets are purposefully set to communicate and measure what an individual, group, school, school district, or management entity is held accountable to achieve in a given performance period. The performance target is the part of a performance objective that focuses precisely on how much or to what extent results will change during the period that will be monitored and measured. For example, for the performance objective "Reduce student absenteeism to three or fewer days by the end of the school year," the performance *target* is "three or fewer days."

Performance targets are often translated into a performance dashboard. Whether web-based, developed as a spreadsheet or table, or posted as simple signs, the dashboard aggregates the key performance indicators of the school, school district, or management entity into easy-to-monitor data points relative to performance targets that provide a snapshot of performance. By keeping this data visible, those involved in supervising and achieving the targeted results can spot and correct negative trends, keep an eye on efficiencies, and identify new trends and changes to inform actions and decisions.

For example, assume a performance dashboard posts weekly and shows that the monthly absenteeism rates are eight days per student three months into the school year. Those accountable for reaching the performance target of less than three days can determine, at a glance, that either what they are doing to reduce student absences is not working or something has happened that is causing a spike in absences and that action is required.

Schools often place these visual reporting tools in their hallways, planning rooms, workrooms, boardrooms, and other places where they can be continually reviewed and analyzed. Many schools and school districts post dashboards on their websites for public review. AdvancEd, an accrediting agency for colleges, universities, and K–12 schools provides ASSIST, a web-based planning tool that helps develop the types of measures and metrics needed for developing an accreditation plan and a performance dashboard. It is available at http://www.advanc-ed.org/platform-assist.

A *Performance Dashboard*, such as the sample shown in Figure 9.1, can be used by a school district to quickly monitor its top performance indicators. Dashboards commonly use a method termed *spotlighting* for easy review of performance statuses. In Figure 9.1, the web-based tool shows a performance flag in green for *On Target*, yellow for *Needs Attention*, and red for *Corrective Action Required*. Clicking on the flag in each achievement category reveals the number of students in each student subpopulation that are contributing to the performance status. Drilling deeper into the performance system's data allows for more comprehensive analysis of the factors contributing to or preventing improvement.

Figure 9.1   Sample Performance Dashboard: Third Grade Students
Exceeding Standards in Math by Subgroups

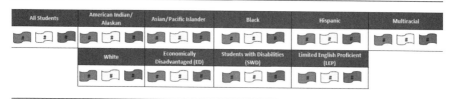

> For a useful dashboard to monitor how students across the
> nation are performing go to http://dashboard.education
> .gov. This dashboard tracks indicators of how students are
> performing from preschool to college and career to meet the
> needs of a global economy. The dashboard allows state and
> national comparisons and understanding of progress and
> change at a glance.

The *Balanced Scorecard*, another strategic management tool, was
developed by David Norton and Robert Kaplan of the Harvard Business
School in the early 1990s. The tool was first used by for-profit organizations to support focused measurement and management of the various
strategies and results that create organizational value, not just financial
measures, thus providing a more balanced view of an organization. The
scorecard has been widely adopted in for-profit organizations, nonprofits,
and the public sector, including many schools. By using the scorecard
to align initiatives to vision and to check performance against strategic
goals, schools use the tool for monitoring, managing, communicating,
and improving performance. The tool reflects the relationships among
team learning and growth; student, team, and stakeholder engagement;
organizational effectiveness; and student achievement (Norton & Kaplan,
1997). Typically, a Balanced Scorecard is developed at the highest level
of the organization, such as the superintendent's office, and is *cascaded*
(developed in alignment to that scorecard) at every level of the school
system and in every support department.

A common failing of organizations in the use of the Balanced
Scorecard is seeing it as an end unto itself. Having a scorecard is not evidence of effective strategic management. Developing and using the tool
to drive implementation of strategies and continuous improvement is an
ongoing journey that promotes dialogue about performance and maintains focus. Developing appropriate measures, metrics, and performance
targets is an ongoing process.

A companion tool to the dashboards and scorecards is the *data room*. Evolving from the notion of a war room used in the military to plan strategy, the data room has developed as a place for posting performance data that inform the daily actions and decisions of those who work in schools. The rooms are typically accessible only to administrators, teachers, and support personnel, and the posted information is organized by major goal areas such as student achievement, organizational effectiveness, engagement by students and stakeholder, and team learning and growth. Posted data drill down to the precise challenges the adults in the school are working to address. Individual cards or posters are arranged to maintain the security of information that often includes students' photos. The data include information that supports the collaboration among the adults in identifying ways to help each student to succeed and to keep the focus on students as unique individuals rather than data points.

Less frequently used but equally important for monitoring are *adoption indicators*—interim results, milestones, and process markers that provide evidence that progress is being made and that people are exhibiting the behaviors they committed to do. By establishing adoption indicators with deadlines before beginning to implement each initiative, those accountable can collect information that maintains focus on implementation and provides feedback to inform actions and decisions. For example, if a set of interventions designed to reduce student absenteeism have been planned, the various adoption indicators might include the following:

- presenting the targeted attendance results and related initiatives at school meetings and school board meetings (first quarter)
- communicating attendance issues and targeted improvements to community leaders and partner organizations (first quarter)
- scheduling and facilitating solution development sessions with stakeholders (first quarter)
- identifying the 20 percent of students with 80 percent of absences (first quarter and annually)
- developing individual plans for chronically absent students (second quarter and annually)
- conducting training sessions for all counselors and 25 percent of the teachers in support interventions for reducing absenteeism (second quarter and annually)
- analyzing scores on student engagement surveys (second quarter and annually)
- making changes in policies and programs that have resulted in students losing instructional time (fourth quarter and annually)

By guiding those accountable for results to keep an eye on whether or not planned actions are being carried out and people are behaving in ways that support the intended outcomes, you can better ensure that all the work that went into facilitating the analysis, diagnosis, and development of solutions translates into the right work and the right sustainable results. Adoption indicators check whether or not the "doing" projected in the planning process is happening. They signal when corrective action is needed. Building in measuring and monitoring processes is critical during the planning and development phase of performance interventions. Taking time to help develop the tools and strategies will enhance your value and reputation as a school improvement facilitator whose work results in fidelity of implementation and sustainability of actions and results, even after you are no longer involved.

Taking Corrective Action

The second element in Standard 9 is about taking corrective action.

9.2 Apply corrective action or refocus efforts, when needed, to reach the targeted performance and results.

Using strategic management tools and setting and monitoring adoption indicators will give you and those you are guiding the information needed to make changes while there is still time to impact outcomes and results. Be sure to include the following:

- agreements to review work status at specific intervals compared to the plan
- protocols for facilitating when deviations occur, to determine if
  - it is worth addressing now
  - what those who can impact the results agree to do
  - who will do what
  - by when
- sticking to meetings and reviews as planned

You may need to help supervisors determine the best course of action when implementation is not proceeding as planned or getting the needed results. Guide them to conduct a root cause analysis of the underperformance or nonperformance, using the same process used to identify the needed interventions. You may find that no serious problems exist and minor changes can get performance back on track, or you may find that a problem statement needs to be developed and that either changes need to be made to the intervention or barriers to performance in the work, workers, or workplace must be addressed.

In the classic Shewhart Cycle of continuous improvement, otherwise known as *The Plan-Do-Check-Act Cycle* (Figure 9.2), applying corrective action and refocusing efforts reflects the *Act* phase of improvement. Since things rarely turn out exactly as imagined and planned, you can help those you are guiding to recognize corrective action, or the *Act* phase, as a natural part of the iterative cycle of improvement and an opportunity to refine interventions or recognize that the causes of performance gaps may not have been adequately identified.

Figure 9.2   The Plan-Do-Check-Act Cycle

Addressing Underperformance

The third element in Standard 9 is about intervening early, not waiting until it is more difficult for corrective action to be effective.

> 9.3 Address underperformance or lack of progress toward goals and performance targets using data and evidence.

Addressing underperformance may be one of the toughest tasks you guide others to do to improve schools. Most administrators and supervisors will tell you that confronting underperformance is the hardest part of their role and often creates more anxiety for the supervisor than the performer. You can help the supervisors you guide to reframe the issue by reflecting on their role, to achieve results through others, and to recognize that their success is supported or limited by the achievement of those they manage and lead. Failure to address underperformance hurts the performer, the school, the students, and the supervisor. Failure to address underperformance is failure to appropriately manage and lead.

By helping supervisors focus on data and evidence of performance that demonstrates what was done or not done and how well, you can help them reduce their anxiety related to addressing performance issues and make them more effective and helpful to those performers for whom they are accountable. If they struggle with this critical skill, your role is to model giving feedback to underperformers, to coach and guide them to appropriately prepare for performance conversations, and to focus on specific observable performance and results, rather than fuzzy attributes like "attitude."

For example, one novice principal explained to his school improvement specialist that one teacher was not only resistant to the new initiatives he was championing but clearly did not respect his leadership. He expressed that he was frustrated because the teachers' attitude was hurting his influence on the faculty. He said he suspected she was angry that he had been promoted into the principal role instead of her. When asked how he knew this to be the case, he responded that he was guessing based on how the teacher was acting.

"Now we are getting somewhere," the specialist encouraged. "Guessing isn't helpful in solving performance issues. We are not investing a crime and establishing motive. We are looking at what is observable and measurable. What have you observed?"

The principal described the teacher's behavior in staff meetings, which included sitting in front of the principal and turning her chair so that her back was facing him. He said she also had not provided the agendas from the learning community she was assigned to lead or any evidence that she had conducted those sessions or had any outputs or deliverables.

The specialist then worked with the principal to prepare to address the performance issue, focusing on the observable, measurable outcomes and performance evidence. They role-played how he would conduct the conversation, how he would communicate what he would accept as evidence that the performance had improved, and what the deadline for improvement would be.

Your role is to coach those you are guiding to be specific, to prepare for performance conversations or progress reviews, and to develop and use protocols for reviewing performance and outcomes. If you can help those who are monitoring the implementation of planned projects and initiatives to maintain professional discipline and build discipline in others to follow through on commitments, that follow-through will increase sustainability.

Sales managers often call this process of reviewing with salespeople what they have done since their last planning session "checking the traps." This refers to the planning, time, and effort a hunter must devote to setting traps in order to catch game. If the traps are set but never checked, the hunter will never know what (if anything) was caught. Part of your role is teaching those who lead the improvement efforts and who are ultimately accountable for the results to regularly "check the traps" to see what has happened since the last *Check* phase in The Plan-Do-Check-Act Cycle so that corrective action can be made or progress can be recognized and reinforced.

Recognizing and Communicating

The fourth element of Standard 9 is about recognizing those who are fulfilling their commitments.

> 9.4 Recognize and communicate about effort, improvement, and achievements.

In addition to conducting regular status checks and keeping the initiatives on the agenda of meetings with your client, you must also encourage those who supervise the adults in the school or school district to recognize people's effort and progress. If you have been effective in facilitating the planning, you have created the opportunity to show progress and improvement evident early in the process. By purposefully identifying those planned tasks that can be accomplished quickly, you can create a sense of momentum and build others' confidence in reaching the goals by focusing their attention on the achievements.

Recognition can be as simple and private as a handwritten note left behind after a classroom observation or as public as a presentation at a school board meeting. Acknowledging others' efforts is key to sustaining commitment. If you or those you are supporting can use milestones as opportunities for communication and recognition as well as "checking the traps," you can balance the pressure of accountability for results with support and reinforcement for those doing the work.

Recognition need not be costly or require resources that will exceed your budget if you do it frequently. For example, search your local beaches, streams, fields, or hardware or craft store for small, smooth stones. A simple handshake or smile and the exchange of a stone with the specific statement of the effort or results and the phrase "You rock!" can mark the achievement of small wins that will add up to a major change and improvement. The recipient may either pass the stone along to colleagues whose achievements he or she wishes to recognize or keep his or her stone as a growing monument to his or her effort and achievement. There is no excuse for not recognizing effort and improvement. If you can find a rock, you can recognize effort and results and encourage those who supervise and lead the work to do the same.

Dr. Rosabeth Moss-Kanter of the Harvard School of Business has extensively researched change management across a wide range of sectors. The Reinventing Education Change Toolkit, available at http://www.reinventingeducation.org, is a free online tool for educators and was developed through a partnership formed by IBM and Kanter, with sponsorship from the Council of Chief State School Officers (CCSSO), the National Association of Secondary School Principals (NAASP), and the National Association of Elementary School Principals (NAESP). The tool draws on Kanter's research, using IBM technology and the deep expertise within sponsor organizations, to provide guidance on facilitating change. The tool's diagnostics can be used to evaluate progress and effectiveness in managing the change process with recommendations of high-leverage practices, such as celebrating "quick wins" in the school improvement process.

The late Theodore Sizer, founder of the Coalition of Essential Schools, studied and wrote extensively about the challenge of improving schools, particularly high schools. One of the central challenges of change and improvement that he identified was that schools must be able to shift as students and their community change and grow. His assertion that when one thing changes, everything must change points to the need for active and persistent focus on implications and impacts and coordination of improvement plans and efforts (Sizer, 1992).

Aligning

The last element of Standard 9 is about confirming the alignment between and across school systems.

> 9.5 Ensure school improvement and transformation is aligned between schools and with the district office or management entity so that schools' efforts support systemwide improvement without undesirable impact on other schools.

The schools you support are the front lines of the improvement and transformation process you facilitate. As you guide changes in the work, workers, and workplace, it is important to remember the systemic nature of the school and its place within the larger context of the school district and the community. No doubt you have heard or provided admonishments to avoid random acts of improvement—well-intentioned efforts and initiatives that are not aligned or work at cross-purposes. Your role as the facilitator of improvement is to help those you are guiding to communicate, collaborate, and coordinate efforts. One of the challenges of empowering people to improve is to provide them a broad enough view into the system of teaching and learning they are impacting to recognize how their efforts relate to others' work.

Dr. Phyllis Edwards is a Certified School Improvement Specialist who led the City Schools of Decatur in Decatur, Georgia, to become the state's first Charter Schools System. This change required each school to establish a local school leadership team (SLT). The SLT is composed of teachers, parents, administrators, and community members, voted onto the SLT by their peers to make key decision for the school site. SLTs assist the district governance team of the board and the superintendent in their work to establish one of the top ten school systems in the nation.

> Becoming a System Charter [School System] required change in the governance structure throughout the system. By empowering each school within the system to make key decisions at the level closest to the students, a sense of engagement in authentic work was established. When designing the charter, which was submitted to and accepted by the State Board of Education, it was imperative that the different levels of governance were given clear guidelines on [their] areas of responsibility. A "no-impact" principle was set forth . . . [to help] the schools to determine if the question they are considering actually sits with their . . . [charter]. Change can be made if the change does not impact another school with the system. In the event that change is recommended that crosses over into other areas of the school system, the charter allowed for the establishment of a Systemwide Charter Leadership Team (SCLT). The SCLT is [composed] . . . of the superintendent and a member of each of the School Leadership Teams. The group meets quarterly to discuss and make recommendation that may affect the school system as a whole. This system increases coordination and avoids unintended consequences. (P. Edwards, personal communication, December 12, 2011)

Penny Smith is a Certified School Improvement Specialist who works with struggling schools in the region where she formerly served as a principal.

> I closely study the schools' improvement plans to get a clear view of what the schools have declared they are doing, and [I] check to see what else they are doing or what they are not doing that needs to be included in the plan. It is also important for me to check these plans for alignment with the district's improvement plan and communicate with others within the school district to ensure

that efforts are aligned. If I find activities or programs that don't show up on any plans and that don't align to any of the goals, my role is to call the question, "Why are you doing this?" If an activity does not align to their goals, it is time to decide if that activity is still necessary and if resources could be better deployed to other priorities. (P. Smith, personal communication, August 17, 2011)

One simple tool that can be used to test for alignment and congruence of efforts is to develop a *Fishbone Diagram,* such as the one used to study root causes, giving each major "bone" the label of a goal in the strategic plan or the school improvement plan (see the *Fishbone Diagram* [Tool 3.3] in Chapter 3). Next, lead the school team to brainstorm every initiative and effort underway in the school and to chart each on the "bone" it supports. When efforts are identified that cannot be matched to any goal area, that initiative is a target for further review to either better align it or to consider it for *selective abandonment,* a choice to forego that effort for higher-value work.

Effective execution is the key to successful school improvement and transformation. The work of Standard 9, to monitor accountability and adoption, is ongoing work. Your job is to support those you have facilitated to master the work of school improvement and continue it past your engagement, so they will achieve the intended results.

A very useful tool for planning and monitoring adoption of the interventions needed to meet improvement goals is the *Logic Chain,* developed by Dr. Judith Hale (see Figure 9.3 and Tool 9.1). This simple tool can be used to plan, facilitate, align, and track implementation to keep people focused on specific results.

Figure 9.3   Logic Chain

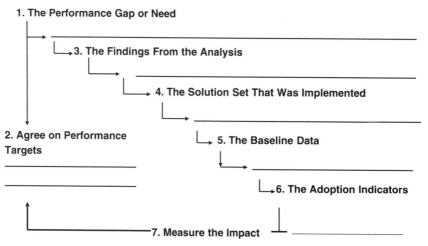

Tool 9.1   Logic Chain

Guidelines: Meet with your team and create a Logic Chain like that shown in Figure 9.3. Facilitate the group in completing the information called for in Section 1 through 7. Use the measures agreed to during the planning phase (see Chapter 4). Facilitate the group in agreeing on what measures it wants to use as adoption indicators for each initiative. Post the chart in an area where everyone can see it, and use it to help monitor progress. The following list explains what information goes in each section of the chart.

1. This is where you put a short statement that expresses the problem and the gap (for example: "Graduation rates are below state standards"). The statement needs to clearly state the problem or opportunity improvement efforts will address.

2. This is where you list the measurable performance targets (for example: "graduation rates of X percent").

3. This is where you briefly list what the analysis uncovered as to the causes of the problem stated in Section 1.

4. This is where you will write down the selected combination of interventions that will be implemented. You want to show the design of a suite of aligned and coordinated interventions in the work, workers, and workplace. The combination incorporates how you plan to improve the work (the job of adults and students), the workers (adult and student capability), and the workplace (the school and learning environment).

5. This is where you put in the baseline data that reflect the current situation (for example: current graduation rates).

6. This where you list the behaviors of adults and students that must be evidenced if progress is to be made. You can also list interim outcomes and outputs, such as presentations to parents and teachers; however, this is what you will monitor at predetermined intervals (perhaps as listed in the milestone report) to determine if progress is being made.

7. This is where you list the changes made at milestones.

AN EXAMPLE OF AN EFFECTIVE APPLICATION OF STANDARD 9

Sydney Turpin worked at the central office of Lowry Schools. At the beginning of the school year, she helped each school leadership team set its performance targets for the year at the school, department, group, and individual levels. Turpin used the Balanced Scorecard that the district office had developed the previous year to facilitate the district leadership in developing a performance dashboard for the district and guided each school to develop its own dashboard and scorecard.

Using the district school improvement plan and each of the schools' improvement plans and project plans for the year, Turpin met with each school leadership team and guided them to build a data room, which had individual student profiles on display. She communicated and established regular progress-reporting meetings in which the teams accountable for carrying out their improvement plans met with her and the superintendent to review their progress and to report on their adoption indicators. Together, she and the superintendent identified positive changes and early improvements, which they reported on the district website, in electronic newsletters, and in a regular segment of the school board's meetings. They encouraged each leadership team to do the same and to report progress at parent-teacher association meetings, faculty meetings, school leadership team meetings, and faculty meetings.

Turpin facilitated each school leadership team in developing its own improvement recognition programs and processes and trained them to use a logic chain to record, monitor, and communicate about their initiatives progress and results. All staff with coaching or supervisory responsibilities was trained in coaching performance, using effective feedback, and addressing underperformance. Together with the principals and central office staff, Turpin guided the design of a process they called "Check and Cheer." These regular progress reviews became opportunities for districtwide collaboration, coordination, and alignment of efforts.

With Turpin's support, principals and leadership teams implemented their own school-based version of the district progress review and recognition process. One school challenged students to bring in empty cereal boxes, such as Cheerios, Chex brand cereals, Total, Special K, and others. Box tops were saved for brands that supported schools, and portions of the boxes were cut out to use as recognition cards, with handwritten notes on the reverse of the portions of the box that contained words that could be used to recognize effort and progress for everyone in the school. Using these and other school-designed processes, monitoring, aligning, and celebrating effort and results became part of the Lowry culture.

AN EXAMPLE OF A LESS EFFECTIVE APPLICATION OF STANDARD 9

Colin Curington was assigned to support a school system to improve its graduation rate. After guiding the district and school staff to review their data, Colin recommended that the school district implement a ninth-grade academy to support middle school to high school transition and reduce dropout rates. Colin led a committee to research other similar interventions and to design the academy and launch it at the start of the next school year.

At the ribbon-cutting ceremony, the group celebrated their project with stakeholders and faculty, and the school board chair praised the group for their efforts. The following week, Colin met with the superintendent and headmaster of the academy. The superintendent said, "I want to thank you both again for your work in planning and launching the academy. Since this was a significant investment for the district and a major change for students, faculty, and staff, we will need to report on the progress made due to this intervention. Also, I want to make sure that the work of the academy is carried out as the research indicates it should be. How will we do that?"

"Honestly, we have been so busy getting this academy developed and open, we have not focused on that," said Colin, "but we can do that next."

"Let's meet next Friday and work on a plan and process for monitoring, reporting, communicating, and addressing any performance issues that we find," replied the superintendent. "I also want to make sure this is a seamless and aligned process with the middle schools and high schools. We are good at planning and doing programs, but we need to be equally good at helping them stick and getting the right results."

REFLECTION

1. What did Turpin do that supported leaders to effectively monitor and manage the work to produce sustainable results?

2. What did Curington do or not do that could interfere with monitoring and keeping the work on track?

3. What in this chapter or in your past experience will be useful when planning and monitoring future initiatives?

POWER POINTS

Here are some suggestions about how to do this work:

- Pay attention to the information that the people really check with regularity, as this is what they are actually monitoring. Pay attention to how they spend their time. For example, if a principal is not checking attendance records or if the assistant principal is not visiting classrooms with the frequency that was agreed on, then the goals of improving attendance or instructional capability are only goals, not commitments. When this happens, raise the issue and ask questions to get people to reflect on their personal priorities and discuss what prevents them from carrying out their commitments.

- Model addressing issues in a timely way, not letting them fester on the hopes the situation will improve without intervention. When you see leaders delay addressing underperformance or lack of progress, do not delay yourself. Use the opportunity to model how to give constructive feedback and reengage others.

- Encourage the school leaders to use the opportunity to align initiatives between schools and with the district office to develop and strengthen their relationships with other leaders in the system. Model for them the behaviors and the benefits of casting a wider net to both learn from others and increase your sphere of influence.

SUMMARY

This chapter has been about continually monitoring people's behavior to confirm that what they are doing is in support of what they say is important. The actions of the leaders, teachers, and administrators reflect their level of commitment to improving performance at all levels. Monitoring adoption starts with agreeing on the actions and behaviors that will give evidence of commitment and follow-through. The next step is to actually monitor and, when necessary, address the need for reengagement or corrective action. Tools such as dashboards, scorecards, and posters help, because they publicize what the leaders have said and show that it is important. However, these tools must be updated at predetermined intervals to communicate the status of the situation. They are excellent tools for reminding everyone of the priorities and reporting on what progress is or is not being made; therefore, they can be used to encourage reflection on what is or is not working. If not used or not used well, they can foster cynicism instead of engagement. Monitoring adoption also means providing leaders with the information they need to recognize those who are fulfilling their commitment and to celebrate every gain and accomplishment. This is a part of a leader's job. It is by monitoring that you and the school leaders will know if there is a need to intervene, to take corrective action, or to celebrate. Monitoring the behaviors of people within the school is only one part. It is equally important to ensure alignment and leverage the available resources by monitoring what other schools in the system are doing and what the district or state leaders are doing.

See the end of this book for a complete list of resources and references related to establishing accountability.

Additional materials and resources related to
The School Improvement Specialist Field Guide
can be found on the companion website.
http://www.corwin.com/sisguide

Implement for Sustainability

10

"It is hard to believe I have been here almost nine months," Bailey Pittman e-mailed Frank Perez. "I really appreciate all the advice you have given me. I am getting a bit anxious because soon my assignment will end, and I want to make sure the work is sustainable after I leave. Any suggestions?"

"Good to hear from you," replied Frank. "I have found that work I have guided is most sustainable when I create processes for helping the leaders of the schools monitor and report their progress regularly and when I have worked deliberately to create ownership by specific individuals. I help them to perceive the work and the results as their efforts, not mine, and to become willing and able to do the work independent of my support. If you want to call me, I can talk you through some of the exact steps I take to make that happen."

"I hope you have been evaluating and documenting the progress and results for the improvement initiatives you are guiding," Frank continued. "It is important that those who assigned you to the school, as well as those you have developed, confirm what has worked and the results they achieved and determine what needs to happen next to sustain progress. It takes three to five years for an underperforming school to reach the critical mass of support, results, and evidence that is needed to move to what I call the 'high-performing zone.' You must help them understand that once you leave, they can use the processes and practices you helped them master to sustain their work and tackle new challenges."

Bailey said, "I want all of us to value what we have learned and achieved. I only have two more weeks here; what do you suggest I do?"

"Take advantage of your remaining reporting meetings to remind them of the value you have added and to get feedback. Then, document your proficiency and theirs and turn it into a success case so others can learn from it. I can share with you the Success Case Method developed by Robert Brinkerhoff, which brings the work to life through a story," Frank said. "You can be proud of your work, and others will learn from your success case."

STANDARD 10: IMPLEMENT FOR SUSTAINABILITY

Standard 10 is about sustaining the behaviors that administrators, teachers, and school leaders learned individually and collectively long enough for them to become institutionalized to the point that they become "the way we do things at this school." In the end, the work of school improvement is about making a difference in the long term while preparing others to sustain the gains made and to continue to work toward transforming teaching and learning to develop the skills students will need to succeed in the 21st century. This requires a long-term commitment. Figure 10.1, *The Implementation and Sustainability Checklist* shows the process that starts by helping everyone at the school gain a deeper understanding of the situation; however, it does not really end at Step 12 with rewarding success, as the work must be ongoing. Sustainability is the successful culmination of all twelve steps. Added to Figure 10.1 are notes that indicate where each essential factor for sustainability has been introduced or described in this book.

Ensuring Continuity

The first element in Standard 10 is about helping school leaders identify what they have to do to sustain the efforts of supporting students,

Figure 10.1   The Implementation and Sustainability Checklist

1. Agree on the goal. (See Chapters 1 and 2.)

2. Agree on baselines performance targets. (See Chapter 2.)

3. Conduct analyses. (See Chapters 2 and 3.)

4. Design, develop, and test the feasibility of the solution set. (See Chapter 4.)

5. Develop a plan to launch and implement the solution set and a sustainability plan. (See Chapters 4, 5, and 6.)

6. Implement focus on the critical mass. (See Chapter 4.)

7. Monitor progress and leading indicators. (See Chapter 9.)

8. Put an oversight structure in place. (See Chapter 7.)

9. Sustain attention by measuring and reporting. (See Chapters 6 and 7.)

10. Reward adoption and results. (See Chapters 9 and 10.)

11. Shift ownership. (See Chapters 7 and 10.)

12. Evaluate and tell your story. (See Chapter 10.)

teachers, and other school leaders and to ensure that the gains that have been made continue to happen. Everyone may know what to do, but the challenge is to keep these things on the agenda and to keep them a priority.

> 10.1 Ensure continuity of interventions, fidelity of execution of plans, and sustainability of gains and improvements.

This element is the culmination of the work you did from the beginning and more. At a minimum, it requires the majority of the people involved in the initiative to commit to continuously analyze the data, revise plans based on new findings and insights, and follow through on those plans. As the school improvement specialist, your role is to confirm that every member of the group has a shared understanding of the work before them both now and in the future. Your role is also to help the group agree and remain clear on who is doing what. It is easy to assume that because the group meets periodically, the work in between the meetings is getting done. Checking on that work and monitoring progress is essential. Fidelity of execution requires carrying out the activities the group agreed were essential for change. It is about fulfilling promises.

From the beginning of an assignment, you facilitated groups in examining the data that reflected their current situation and then in exploring and coming to agreement on what to do to improve student achievement and teacher and leader performance. You modeled the behaviors for coaching and influencing people individually and collectively, so they can contribute to the solution and carry out that commitment. You also modeled how to facilitate groups as they discuss and weigh different courses of action and how to constructively address barriers and resistance, building a critical mass of support and engagement. Tools to support that work were introduced earlier in this book. You can continue to use those tools to foster ongoing engagement.

Transferring Ownership

The second element of Standard 10 is about getting teachers, teacher leaders, and school leaders to assume responsibility for the improvement initiatives and not wait for you to raise the question, ask for the data, or remind others of previous commitments.

> 10.2 Establish and transfer ownership.

The work of the school improvement specialist is to build capability within the ranks of teachers, teacher leaders, and school leaders. School improvement may start with outside intervention, but it is not sustainable if requires long-term assistance. Sustained improvement requires school leaders to recognize that it is their responsibility and role to facilitate setting goals, developing plans to accomplish those goals, and monitoring to confirm that the plans are being carried out. It is also their role to evaluate whether or not the plans are effective and facilitate corrective action as required.

In order to transfer ownership, identify early on who will be accountable to lead the work and who will need to follow up, follow through, and maintain the discipline to implement with fidelity. Invest time and effort in developing those individuals' capability and ownership. Help leaders to identify who they can depend upon to assume ownership and responsibility. Since new projects will inevitably be needed, administrators must be guided to distribute leadership among members of the school team so that improvement projects gradually produce daily work routines resulting in improved practices and results.

Facilitating Evaluation

The third element of Standard 10 is about actually evaluating the work and what was accomplished.

10.3 Facilitate evaluation of the effort.

Your role is to facilitate others in doing the evaluation, not to do it yourself. What needs to be evaluated was ideally decided when you facilitated the group in studying performance data and setting interim and summative performance targets. The basis for the evaluation can be done in the following interdependent ways:

- Gains—This is looking at what has changed and how much it has changed. Your role is to facilitate the group in comparing where the school was when the work began to where it is at specific points in time, such as semiannually or annually. Then, explicitly call out the gains made and ask, "Is this enough?"
- Goal Accomplishment—This is about comparing the gains made to targets or goals set by the group. Your role is to facilitate the group in comparing the gains made at specific points in time to target numbers, such as those provided by government agencies or key constituents. Next, ask the group why they believe they are or are not achieving the goals or meeting targets. Follow up by asking what they need to continue to do or do differently to sustain the gains made and increase the odds of accomplishing their goals.
- Return on Investment—This is about determining the degree to which the investment in a solution or a combination of solutions was worth the effort. This method requires you to facilitate the

group in evaluating the value of the strategies, plans, technologies, and initiatives that were implemented to improve performance of students, teachers, and leaders compared to the gains made. Value does not have to be expressed in dollars. It can be expressed in the time and energy consumed and in the level of acceptability or resistance garnered or not garnered compared to the gains made. The purpose is to help judge if the road taken was the best road compared to the gains made and whether or not it is wise to continue down the same road. It presumes other roads are possible and were considered and rejected.

- Performance—This is about examining multiple factors that collectively reflect the performance of the whole school. This method requires you to facilitate an examination of data for multiple goals, as school performance is about many things. For example, school performance goals can include (1) student achievement in math, reading, and science; (2) teacher capability in instructional delivery; (3) the outcomes of implementing project-based learning assignments to increase student readiness for the workforce; and (4) leader capability in instructional coaching, community involvement, and innovative discipline.

Each of these methods is cumulative and their answers help guide future work. Use the *Evaluations Strategies* tool (Tool 10.1) to help document your evaluation strategy and metrics.

At the beginning of her assignment, school improvement specialist, Rita Tanner, met with the superintendent and three principals to discuss and decide on an evaluation strategy for the work. During the meeting, Rita facilitated the discussion, occasionally raising questions about if and where performance targets would be helpful, if and where alignment to strategic plan goals was needed, on what basis they could judge the value of an initiative, and what factors they wanted to focus on to evaluate the overall performance of the schools in the system. The group developed a chart to record their decisions on what metrics to use. They decided to measure overall school performance against four variables: (1) student achievement in math, reading, and science using standard test scores; (2) school safety, as measured in number of incidents or complaints and the need for intervention by authorities; (3) student readiness, as measured by graduation rates and the number of students going on to advanced study at trade schools, community schools, or four-year colleges; and (4) teacher performance, as measured in increased incidents of adopting recommended instructional tactics, reduced need for instructional coaching, and increased compliance with teaching standards. The group then set goals for each variable and discussed the need to measure enabling behaviors and tactics that they believed would contribute to the achievement of the goals and the overall performance of each school. The group used this strategy to help present data about the school, set targets with the appropriate groups, and lead discussions about how frequently they wanted to meet to discuss gains. They also posted the decisions on the school's website and agreed to update the data at agreed-on times.

Tool 10.1   Evaluation Strategies

Guidelines: To use the *Evaluation Strategies* tool, agree on what you want to evaluate (gains, goal accomplishment, Return on Investment (ROI), or performance). Next, create a column to record your beginning values. Next, decide how often you want to record and report on improvements. Finally, decide (1) how you plan on using the tool, (2) what evaluation methods you want to use, (3) how you will use the results, and (4) to whom and how you want to report what you record.

List Metrics to Be Tracked	Beginning Values	Insert Values at Prescribed Time Periods			
Performance		6 Months	12 Months	18 Months	24 Months
Test scores by class level • Math • Reading • Science • More					
Safety by school • Incidents • More					
Readiness by school • Graduation • Career • Community college • Four-year college					
Teacher capability by class, topic, or school • Coaching • Compliance • Instructional tactics • More					

Gains by class or school • Variable 1 • Variable 2 • Variable 3 • Other					
Goal accomplishment by class or school • Goal 1 • Goal 2					
ROI by school					
Initiative 1 • Time • Cost • Effectiveness • Other					
Initiative 2 • Time • Cost • Effectiveness • Other					

Brinkerhoff (2002) developed the *Success Case Method* for evaluation, which combines storytelling with rigorous evaluation methods and principles. Success cases cite solid evidence. These cases document verifiable and confirmable accounts of what real people experienced, using specific tools and methods. Success cases provide evidence to answer the following key questions about an initiative:

1. What is really happening?

2. What results are being achieved?

3. What is the value of the results?

4. How can it be improved?

Gaining Commitment

The fourth element of Standard 10 is about preparing students for the 21st century. It presumes that schools must improve in student achievement scores and teacher and leader capability but understands that schools also want to focus on building the decision-making and communication skills required for students to be employable in the future.

10.4 Allow time for and gain support for long-term, sustainable improvement and transformation to meet 21st-century needs.

To facilitate the group in evaluating how well it is preparing students for the 21st century, you must help the school teachers and leaders

- identify the skills they want to develop.
- agree on initiatives, programs, or teaching methods that will be used to develop those skills.
- agree on what they will accept as evidence of goal accomplishment.
- agree on how the data will be collected and who will collect the data.
- agree on when they will capture and report on the data.

The three school principals and the superintendent told Rita Tanner that they wanted to develop students' 21st-century skills. Rita told them, "The process for meeting students' needs for future success is much the same as the process used to improve an underperforming school and requires a shared understanding of what skills students will need to be successful not only in academics but in their professional, family, and civic lives. Many good resources already exist for analyzing the gaps between where a school or school district is and where it needs to be to develop higher-order thinking skills, complex communication skills, collaboration skills, and creativity. The Partnership for 21st Century Skills (http://www.P21.org) provides a free assessment tool, *The MILE Guide* (available at http://p21.org/storage/documents/MILE_Guide_091101 .pdf), that helps diagnose what practice, policies, and resources are needed to transform the prevailing model of schooling into a learning organization that supports success for all in the future. The cycle of inquiry and improvement is the same but with the goals focused upon a desired future state of the school or schools preparing students for future success. Working with employers is critical to identify the performance goals for students as well as the skills they need to develop during their K–12 experience.

Improving Continuously

The final element of Standard 10 is about how you will evaluate your ability to facilitate others in the work of school improvement.

10.5 Solicit feedback to evaluate your own performance, and set goals for your own continued development.

One ultimate measure of your effectiveness is your ability to build capability in others, in their ability to do the work without your guidance. Another measure is your effectiveness in facilitating work that results in improvement in specific student achievement performance targets. Other measures might include your effectiveness in facilitating schools to achieve their goals. You can use the *Evidence of Increasing Capacity and Capability* tool (Tool 10.2) to list the factors you want to use to evaluate your effectiveness. You will find the electronic portfolio at http://www.accreditedportfolios.com used by Certified School Improvement Specialists helpful to aggregate and share your evidence for each factor.

As a school improvement specialist and a performance consultant, you can increase your value if you remember to do the following:

- **Define** in advance the value you will add through the work you do, being clear and specific about the outcomes, results, and goals that you will help those you guide to achieve.
- **Promise** the above value both verbally and in writing to those you guide and those who employ your services, clearly stating that you are committed to their success.
- **Deliver** what you have promised and more, guiding others to perform effectively, to achieve the performance targets, and to constantly evaluate progress and your effectiveness as an improvement specialist.
- **Remind** those you guide and serve of the milestones, results, goals, and performance targets achieved through regular updates, individual handwritten notes, e-mails, electronic newsletters, meetings, and other frequent, planned forms of communication that help others to regard you as a valuable resource and themselves as successful professionals. Posing reflective questions in your communications helps you and those you support to recognize the value that has been created, to develop a greater sense of professionalism and efficacy, and to extract meaning from the improvement experiences that you have shared to inform future practice and professional development.

Becoming an effective school improvement specialist who is skilled as a performance consultant is an ongoing process. The process of applying for certification as a Certified School Improvement Specialist (CSIS) is in itself a powerful reflective, developmental process that will help you continue to grow in this valuable profession. Like continuous school improvement processes, there is always room for growth and learning as a CSIS. By continuously evaluating your impact and results, you will continue to

Tool 10.2   Evidence of Increasing Capacity and Capability

Guidelines: To use this tool, first identify the factors related to your own performance that you want to evaluate; examples may include your ability to increase leaders' capability to lead school improvement efforts independently, the number of teachers who improved their instructional capability, the number of self-directed teams that continue to be effective without either your support or involvement, and the gains made and the goals accomplished by a school. For each factor, cite the evidence you believe speaks to your ability. You may edit the factors to match your assignment.

Factor to Evaluate	1st year	2nd year	3rd year
Increased Capability			
Number of school leaders that assumed increasing responsibility for the work of school improvement			
(Cite names and evidence.)			
Number of school leaders whose capability to interpret data improved			
(Cite names and evidence.)			
Number of teachers that took responsibility for improving their instructional tactics			
(Cite names and evidence.)			
Number of teachers whose instructional capability improved			
(Cite names and evidence.)			
Number of self-directed teams			
(Cite examples and evidence.)			
School goals accomplished			
Graduation rates			
Student retention rates			
School safety			
Other			
(Cite examples and evidence.)			
21st-century skills initiatives			
(Cite example and evidence.)			
Other			

grow and to evolve skills that support not only improvement of schools as they comply with expectations but that truly transform schools to meet the needs of their students, their communities, and the world.

AN EXAMPLE OF AN EFFECTIVE APPLICATION OF STANDARD 10

Nick Esperanza was promoted to his first job as principal. His excitement at receiving the promotion was quickly replaced by the realization that the school he was assigned had struggled for over a decade to reach expected levels of student performance. Upon arriving at the school, he was pleased to find an experienced school improvement specialist, Jonnie Hoover, who had been working with the school for the last two years. He scheduled a series of meetings with Hoover, during which they reviewed the data, the interventions that were underway, and the results to date. After reviewing the data and other information, it was clear that the school was, at last, making progress. Hoover told him, "My assignment here will end at the end of this school year. Over the last two years, the retiring principal and I were able to get the team moving in the right direction, but we did not have enough time to make some of the critical changes. If you want my help, I will commit to you to help build your capacity to lead this school to meet its goal and to help you become a highly effective principal. We have momentum and need to sustain it."

Esperanza told her that he was eager for her support and asked what the next steps could be to support the changes and improvements that were underway.

"We need for you to let the other administrators, faculty, and staff know that you are committed to the plan that has been developed and the interventions that are underway," Hoover replied. "There are several things that you can do right away that will let people know you are monitoring and actively supporting the new work they have been trained to do. I can work with you to develop and use a monitoring and support process that will ensure the interventions are implemented with fidelity, and you can keep the team and your supervisors informed of progress. We are nearing a critical mass of teachers who have adopted the new practices they were taught. I will work with you to target those who can help you get to the tipping point, where enough folks are on board and doing the right work that they influence others to support and adopt the changes."

"My role, as I see it," she continued, "is to build your capacity and to support your success as the leader of improvement and transformation in this school as you and your teams equip students to be successful in academics, the world of work, and their family and civic lives long after my assignment here ends. I see your role as building capacity and ownership in the work by supporting those who work in the school so that improved practices and a culture of high performance becomes 'how things are done around here' and the team will own the work and results."

Hoover handed him a folder, "This is a copy of the school improvement plan and the various project plans for the initiatives underway. I have developed an aligned set of goals for myself for the year (which I want to review with you) and a process for evaluating and reporting on progress. If we can align our goals and use the evaluation data, feedback, and information to inform each other, the team, and your supervisors, then we can prove that we are driving the right changes and we can provide evidence of progress and improvement. You will notice that I have collected two years of data and evidence of how my facilitation of the work here has impacted each year's results and goals. I am working to earn an evidence-based Certified School Improvement Specialist job certification, using my performance evidence and school performance data. If you are interested, I can share the CSIS standards with you and help you build a portfolio of evidence. By end of the school year, I want you to be both comfortable and effective in your role here and able to sustain the work in progress and reach the school's goals and your own."

She concluded, "You see, I am only successful if you are successful and if the work and improvement is sustained after my time here is over. I am very committed to your success, and I promise to help you in every way I possibly can, if you are committed to this shared work and to continuously improving what those who work in the school do. Our challenge, in addition to helping this school meet the standards, is to exceed the standards and transform the school to meet the needs of students in the 21st century. I will do all I can to help you successfully lead this school forward, if you want my support."

Esperanza confirmed that he wanted her support and communicated at the staff meeting later that day that he was committed to continuity of the improvement efforts and to working with Hoover and the team to take the school to levels of performance that would far exceed the minimum expectations for compliance with mandates. He further committed to helping the school team create a 21st-century learning environment, where both adults and students were learning together, solving real-world problems, building on their strengths, and innovating better ways to work and learn together.

AN EXAMPLE OF A LESS EFFECTIVE APPLICATION OF STANDARD 10

"I think I have whiplash from changing programs so often," joked Jody Ekard, head of the science department at Jackson City Schools, to a newly assigned school improvement specialist at her school. "We have had three different instructional coaches, two different school improvement specialists, and two different principals in the last four years. Every one brought a new set of programs, projects, and initiatives designed to improve our students' performance. The problem was that we were constantly in start-up mode with programs and never had the chance to see anything through fully. I have been teaching here for over 20 years. I fully understand that as research reveals more about how students learn and the instructional practices that support higher-order thinking skills and long-term academic success, we should adapt our teaching practices, but at some point, enough is enough. Let's just do something and stick to it. And for once, I'd like to be involved in designing the solutions, rather than having someone tell me we have to do a new program. As the department chair, I feel I have the responsibility to build ownership among the science faculty for changes, but it is hard to do that when things are changing constantly. I am a realist, and I know that our practices must evolve and improve, but the 'program of the month' mentality here is impeding the type of genuine change and improvement that will truly help our team and students be successful."

REFLECTION

1. What did Hoover and Esperanza do that increased the likelihood that their efforts would result in the needed improvements?

2. What was going on at Jackson City Schools that was impeding progress? What could have been done to ensure that the schools initiatives were sustainable and successful in the long term?

3. What would you do differently in the future, based on what you learned from your past experiences or from this chapter?

4. What tools in this chapter might be helpful in sustaining the projects and results you facilitate, even when you are no longer actively involved?

POWER POINTS

Here are some suggestions for implementing for sustainability.

- Share Figure 10.1, *The Implementation and Sustainability Checklist* with your school leaders, and use it as a basis to discuss how well they are prepared to sustain the gains they have made. Have them identify where they think they need to improve to better ensure that their efforts continue long enough to reap the desired long-term benefits. Use their insights to guide them in identifying what they can do to increase the odds that the gains made through their efforts are sustained.
- To evaluate how well you have transferred ownership of the process to school leaders, pay attention to the number of times they initiate ideas and follow up on initiatives without prompting by you.
- To learn more about how to develop the skills required for the 21st century, visit http://www.p21.org.

SUMMARY

The standard on which this chapter is based is about shifting the responsibility for school improvement to the people who eventually must own it if they want to sustain any gains in student, teacher, or leader performance. It is also about the importance of building the capability to improve the performance of students, teachers, and leaders to the people who work within school systems. Finally, this chapter is the culmination of the previous chapters, as it builds on the skills you have developed in yourself and in others through the ideas and tools presented earlier.

See the end of the book for a complete list of resources and references related to implementation of major initiatives.

Additional materials and resources related to
The School Improvement Specialist Field Guide
can be found on the companion website.
http://www.corwin.com/sisguide

Readiness Assessment

This assessment is intended to help you reflect on your areas of strength and areas for improvement. You may want to share your observations with others who know your work, as they may see strengths and areas for improvement that you have overlooked. Use the results as input to create your own development plan and to assess your readiness to apply for the Certified School Improvement Specialist (CSIS) certification.

STANDARD 1: ANALYZE AND APPLY CRITICAL JUDGMENT

A. How proficient are you in your ability to analyze qualitative and quantitative data to determine performance gaps?

B. How proficient are you in your ability to validate data?

C. How proficient are you in your ability to observe instruction in order to collect more complete data to help you assess performance?

D. How proficient are you in using data-gathering tools and protocols that help you stay focused, avoid judging prematurely, and be consistent in your approach?

E. How proficient are you in facilitating others to accurately interpret data?

F. How proficient are you in presenting data, so others recognize the implications?

G. How proficient are you in initially creating trust, building credibility, and demonstrating value to those you facilitate?

H. What evidence can you provide of your proficiency in *Standard 1: Analyze and Apply Critical Judgment,* based on improvement work you have guided in the past three years?

I. What data can you provide that shows a cause-and-effect relationship between your performance of the work of Standard 1 and improvements in the work, workers, and workplace of a school or schools?

STANDARD 2: FACILITATE DERIVING MEANING AND ENGAGEMENT

A. How proficient are you in your ability to help groups identify factors about the following:

1. Work—how the work is designed, the adequacy and efficiency of the procedures, the clarity and reasonableness of the deliverables or expectations, the adequacy of the resources, and so on

2. Workers—how skilled the players are (superintendents, principals, teacher leaders, teachers, and others) and how motivated they are to support the needed changes

3. Workplace—the consistency of direction from leaders and the adequacy of the school or school system's infrastructure (facilities, equipment, information systems, incentive practices, etc.)

4. External environment—the dependability and adequacy of support from community leaders, families, and others

B. How proficient are you in your ability to facilitate the use of the tools in Chapter 2, especially the ones designed to lead people to recognize the implications of their decisions?

C. How proficient are you in your ability to use techniques designed to assure that everyone feels that his or her opinion was respectfully considered, to control dominant personalities in the groups, and to structure working sessions so that everyone is focused on the important work?

D. How proficient have you been in building support and peer networks?

E. What evidence, supported by multiple types of data from the last three years, do you have to prove your proficiency in Standard 2?

F. Where might you get coaching to improve your ability to facilitate others in doing the work described in Chapter 2?

STANDARD 3: FOCUS ON SYSTEMIC FACTORS

A. How proficient are you in your ability to help groups focus on the systemic factors that affect student, teacher, and leader performance?

B. How proficient are you in your ability to guide the group in identifying and selecting interventions designed to improve people's performance?

C. How proficient are you in your ability to guide the group in identifying and selecting interventions designed to improve the work people do?

D. How proficient are you in your ability to guide the group in identifying and selecting interventions designed to improve the workplace?

E. How proficient are you in your ability to facilitate the use of the tools in Chapter 3, especially the ones designed to help people select an appropriate suite or menu of interventions?

F. How proficient are you in your ability to guide the group in identifying both opportunities and methods to develop 21st-century skills?

G. What evidence, supported by multiple types of data from the last three years, do you have to prove your proficiency in Standard 3?

H. Where might you get coaching to improve your ability to facilitate others in doing the work described in Chapter 3?

STANDARD 4: PLAN AND RECORD

A. How proficient are you in your ability to lead others in assessing the feasibility of a course of action?

B. How proficient are you in your ability to lead others in developing a project charter?

C. How proficient are you in your ability to develop action plans?

D. How proficient are you in your ability to explain the hierarchy of plans and what each level is expected to accomplish?

E. How proficient are you in the use of the *Communications Worksheet* (Tool 4.5) to help your team recognize the importance of keeping others informed and how to best do it?

F. How proficient are you in the use of a *Milestone Report* (Tool 5.2) to help your team recognize the importance of reporting accomplishments?

G. What evidence, supported by multiple types of data from the last three years, do you have to prove your proficiency in Standard 4?

H. Where might you get coaching to improve your ability to facilitate others in doing the work described in Chapter 4?

STANDARD 5: ORGANIZE AND MANAGE EFFORTS AND RESOURCES

A. How proficient are you in your ability to break down work into manageable steps so that others see the work as doable?

B. How proficient are you in distributing the work so that others develop the skills and proficiency to assume responsibility for the outcomes?

C. How proficient are you in coordinating multiple teams and projects?

D. How proficient are you in using project management tools to keep others engaged and committed to meeting the agreed-on outcomes?

E. What evidence, supported by multiple types of data from the last three years, do you have to prove your proficiency in Standard 5?

F. What can you do to strengthen your skills in this area?

STANDARD 6: GUIDE AND FOCUS COLLABORATIVE IMPROVEMENT

A. How proficient are you in your ability to leverage your relationships with peers and people you know at work or who work with your client?

B. Which of the following requests are easy and which are hard for you to do: ask for information, ask for feedback, ask for counsel, or ask for someone to introduce you to others?

C. How proficient are you in your ability to establish a wider circle of influence?

D. How proficient are you in your ability to help others select the measures that are aligned with the performance indicators, thus ensuring the group is on the right track?

E. How proficient are you in your ability to stay in the know when it comes to offering colleagues information they can use when it would be most helpful?

F. How proficient are you in your ability to model the behaviors you want to see in others?

G. How proficient are you in helping others ask the hard questions?

H. What evidence, supported by multiple types of data from the last three years, do you have to prove your proficiency in Standard 6?

I. Where might you get coaching on how to facilitate others to do the work in this standard?

STANDARD 7: BUILD CAPACITY

A. How proficient are you in your ability to use adult learning theory to build capacity in others?

B. How proficient are you at developing learning and development interventions that improve the performance of those carrying out the work of school improvement?

C. How proficient are you in modeling, setting expectations, and giving feedback so that leaders can more effectively direct the work of others?

D. How proficient are you at helping leaders define core competencies and then structure their hiring and talent management practices to attract people with those competencies?

E. What evidence, supported by multiple types of data from the last three years, do you have to prove your proficiency in Standard 7?

F. What might you do to strengthen your skills in this area?

STANDARD 8: DEMONSTRATE ORGANIZATIONAL SENSITIVITY

A. Rate yourself on a scale of 1 (Very Good) to 5 (Needs Help) for the following attributes:

Attributes	1 Very Good	2 Good	3 Not Sure	4 Not Consistent	5 Needs Help	Comments
Can you quickly establish rapport with others?						
Can you quickly gain others' trust?						
Are you described by others as credible?						
Are you aware of the social norms of the groups you interact with?						
Do you monitor your own behavior so it better matches the groups' norms?						
Do you periodically check your own appearance to confirm that it supports how you want to be seen?						
Do you take the time to check your writing to confirm that it is clear and well written?						
Do you reach out to make sure everyone is engaged?						
Do you confirm your own interpretation of what you hear or observe?						
Are you skilled at noticing group interactions?						
Can you confirm that people regard you as credible?						

B. What evidence, supported by multiple types of data from the last three years, do you have to prove your proficiency in Standard 8?

C. What might you do to strengthen your skills in this area?

STANDARD 9: MONITOR ACCOUNTABILITY AND ADOPTION

A. How proficient are you in your ability to help team members identify what behaviors to observe or interim results to monitor?

B. How proficient are you in your ability to facilitate leaders in recognizing when corrective action is warranted and how to best take that action?

C. How proficient are you in your ability to coach leaders in how to prepare to give feedback and how to have conversations during which they can cite specific behaviors or results that have to be stopped, started, or improved?

D. How proficient are you in your ability to help leaders find ways to acknowledge improvements?

E. How proficient are you in your ability to help people confirm that their performance improvement efforts are aligned with what other schools are doing?

F. How proficient are you in your ability to help leaders assess how their initiatives might impact other schools or other performance improvement programs?

G. What evidence, supported by multiple types of data from the last three years, do you have to prove your proficiency in Standard 9?

H. What might you do to strengthen your skills in this area?

STANDARD 10: IMPLEMENT FOR SUSTAINABILITY

A. How proficient are you in your ability to use the tools in Chapter 10 to help others continue to measure the right things, so their efforts are sustained long enough to reap the benefits?

B. How proficient are you in your ability to let go, so others can step up and assume responsibility for the work ahead?

C. How proficient are you in your ability to use adoption indicators to encourage continued engagement and celebrate successes and gains?

D. How proficient are you in your ability to facilitate others in finding and committing to practices that build 21st-century skills?

E. What evidence, supported by multiple types of data from the last three years, do you have to prove your proficiency in Standard 10?

F. What might you do to strengthen your skills in this area?

Resources Listed by Chapter

Chapter 1

The following publications offer practical advice about analyzing and presenting data:

Coggins, C. T., Stoddard, P., & Cutler, E. (2003, April). *Improving instructional capacity through school-based reform coaches.* Paper presented at the Annual Meeting of the American Educational Research Association, Chicago, IL.

Guerra-Lopez, I. J. (2008). *Performance evaluation: Proven approaches for improving program and organizational performance.* San Francisco, CA: Jossey-Bass.

Henry, G. T. (1995). *Graphing data: Techniques for display and analysis.* Thousand Oaks, CA: Sage.

Kaufman, R. A., Guerra, I., & Platt, W. A. (2006). *Practical evaluation for educators: Finding what works and what doesn't.* Thousand Oaks, CA: Corwin.

Chapter 2

The following website provides more information, tools, and support for Joel Barker's implications mapping:

Barker, J. (2011). The implications wheel [Website]. Retrieved from http://www.implicationswheel.com

The following book is a useful and easy-to-use guide for leading groups in school improvement.

Conzemius, A., & O'Neill, J. (2002). *The handbook for smart school teams.* Bloomington, IN: National Educational Service.

This book is full of inspiring examples of people making a difference in the lives of others. Frances Hesselbein is the chairperson and founding president of the Peter F. Drucker Foundation. She also is a former CEO of the Girl Scouts of America.

Hesselbein, F. (2002). *Hesselbein on leadership.* San Francisco, CA: Jossey-Bass.

This pocket-sized guide contains useful tools and practices for supporting and facilitating school improvement.

Magnus, A. (1992). *The memory jogger for education: A pocket guide for continuous improvement in schools.* Salem, NH: GOAL/QPC.

Whitney, D., Trosten-Bloom, A., & Rader, K. (2010). *Appreciative leadership: Focus on what works to drive winning performance and build a thriving organization.* New York, NY: McGraw-Hill.

The following publications offer research related to controlling group dynamics:

Cooperrider, D. L., & Whitney, D. K. (2005). *Appreciative inquiry: A positive revolution in change.* San Francisco, CA: Berrett-Koehler.

Debecq, A. L., Van de Ven, A. H., & Gustafson, D. H. (1975). *Group techniques for program planning: A guide to nominal group and Delphi processes.* Glenview, IL: Scott Foresman.

This seminal research is excellent reading. Nominal Group Technique (NGT) was developed to mitigate the influence of group members who have greater positional power or are perceived as having greater social power. The goal was to improve groups' decision making, specifically by reducing powerful personalities' influence over the group's ability to generate and impartially examine ideas. The word *nominal* implies the people in the group are a group in name only; they do not necessarily work together or otherwise function as a group outside of this particular situation. NGT is an effective technique for generating a comprehensive set of facts and weighing those facts according to some variable, such as importance or frequency. Because responses are assigned points, you can identify those responses that are statistically significant.

Greenbaum, T. L. (1998). *The practical handbook and guide to focus group research.* Lexington, MA: Lexington Books.

Hayes, T. J., & Tatham, C. B. (1989). *Focus group interviews: A reader* (2nd ed.). Chicago, IL: American Marketing Association.

Tichy, N. M., & Cohen, E. B. (2002). *The leadership engine: How winning companies build leaders at every level.* New York, NY: HarperBusiness.

Toseland, R. W., Rivas, R. F., & Chapman, D. (1984, July/August). An evaluation of decision-making methods in task groups. *Social Work, 29*(4), 339–346.

Watkins, J. M., & Mohr, B. J. (2001). *Appreciative inquiry: Change at the speed of imagination.* San Francisco, CA: Jossey-Bass.

Chapter 3

Carl Binder PhD, Certified Performance Technologist, developed a model for diagnosing performance problems, prioritizing them, and selecting interventions. Go to http://www.sixboxes.com to find more about his work.

Binder, C. (2010). Six boxes: Performance thinking [Website]. Retrieved from http://www.sixboxes.com

The website, http://www.p21.org, published by Partnership for 21st Century Skills (P21) contains information and tools to support 21st-century skills. Explore the 4 Cs: Creativity, Communication, Collaboration, and Critical Thinking; and the 21st Century Skills Framework. P21 has developed a free assessment, the MILE Guide, to systematically analyze the gap between current and best practices for 21st-century transformation.

Partnership for 21st Century Skills. (2011). [Website]. Retrieved from http://www.p21.org

Deb Wagner developed a human performance technology toolkit, which you can get at http://debwagner.info/hpttoolkit/instr_hpt.htm.

Wagner, D. (n.d.). HPT toolkit: A resource for human performance technologists [Website]. Retrieved from http://debwagner.info/hpttoolkit/instr_hpt.htm

This book introduces human performance technology. It is an excellent source of information and tools especially designed to improve performance in the workplace. The third edition of this book, released in May 2012, is titled *Fundamentals of Performance Improvement: A Guide to Improving People, Process, and Performance.*

Van Tiem, D. M., Moseley, J. L., & Dessinger, J. C. (2004). *Fundamentals of performance technology: A guide to improving people, process, and performance* (2nd ed.). Silver Springs, MD: International Society for Performance Improvement.

Chapter 4

The American Management Association offers courses in project management. Go to http://www.amanet.org/ for more information.

American Management Association. (2012). [Website]. Retrieved from http://www.amanet.org/

Commitment-based project management (CBPM) has evolved from a performance-based perspective on project management. Information and resources relevant to this approach are available at http://www .ensemblemc.com. Their emphasis is on ensuring that each team member understands how his or her part supports the whole project. Team members participate in defining who needs to deliver what to whom by when in order to achieve the project goals. Instead of working against task estimates, team members turn their deliverables into short-interval, personal commitments that they monitor (as *done* or *not done*) on a weekly basis. As the project evolves, team members take responsibility to proactively renegotiate commitments to each other in order to stay on track to goals. The school improvement specialist facilitates these practices and ensures that trade-off decisions are transparent and addressed at the appropriate level of authority. The method has been proven to improve schedule reliability and quality of outputs on both large and small projects.

Ensemble Management Consulting. (2012). [Website]. Retrieved from http://www.ensemblemc.com

This website, http://www.pmi.org, published by the Project Management Institute, is an excellent source for learning the craft of project management and for obtaining information on earning a project manager credential.

Project Management Institute. (2012). [Website]. Retrieved from http://www.pmi.org

An Internet search provides numerous tools and resources to support project planning. For example, you can find a sample electronic project plan template in Microsoft Office Word format at http://www .Office.com using the Templates link.

Microsoft Project is a useful software application for managing large and complex initiatives. It allows you to display the major headings, such as initiatives and individual tasks. In addition, it allows you to specify the resources required for each task and to describe how and if one step depends on another step before that step can be started. The application comes with tutorials to guide you through every step of the planning process.

Microsoft Excel can be used effectively for project planning and budgeting.

Chapter 5

Pink, D. H. (2009). *Drive: The surprising truth about what motivates us.* New York, NY: Riverhead Books.

Portny, S. E. (2010). *Project management for dummies* (3rd ed.). Hoboken, NJ: Wiley Publishing.

Chapter 6

Bellanca, J., & Brandt, R. (Eds.). (2010). *21st century skills: Rethinking how students learn.* Bloomington, IN: Solution Tree Press.

National School Boards Association. (2009). The Center for Public Education [Website]. Retrieved from http://www.centerforpubliceducation .org

Poister, T. H. (2003). *Measuring performance in public and nonprofit organizations.* San Francisco, CA: Jossey-Bass.

Trilling, B., & Fadel, C. (2009). *21st century skills: Learning for life in our times.* San Francisco, CA: Jossey-Bass.

Chapter 7

DuFour, R., Eaker, R., & DuFour, R. (2008). *Revisiting professional learning communities at work: New insights for improving schools.* Bloomington, IN: Solution Tree.

Foshay, W. R., Silber, K. H., & Stelnicki, M. B. (2003). *Writing training materials that work: How to train anyone to do anything.* San Francisco, CA: Jossey-Bass/Pfeiffer.

Gery, G. J. (1999). Electronic performance support system (EPSS). In D. J. Langdon, K. S. Whiteside, & M. M. McKenna (Eds.), *Intervention resource guide: 50 performance improvement tools* (pp. 142–148). San Francisco, CA: Jossey Bass/Pfeiffer.

Merriam, S. B., Caffarella, R. S., & Baumgartner, L. M. (2007). *Learning in adulthood: A comprehensive guide* (3rd ed.). San Francisco, CA: Jossey-Bass.

Rossett, A. (1996). Job aids and electronic performance support systems. In R. L. Craig (Ed.), *The ASTD training & development handbook: A guide to human resource development* (4th ed., pp. 557–578). New York, NY: McGraw-Hill.

Stevens, E. F., & Stevens, G. H. (1995). *Designing electronic performance support tools: Improving workplace performance with hypertext, hypermedia and multimedia.* Englewood Cliffs, NJ: Educational Technology Publications.

Villachica, S. W., & Stone, D. L. (1999). Performance support systems. In H. D. Stolovitch & E. J. Keeps (Eds.), *Handbook of human performance technology: Improving organizational performance worldwide* (2nd ed., pp. 441–463). San Francisco, CA: Jossey Bass/Pfeiffer/ISPI.

Winer, L. R., Rushby, N., & Vazquez-Abad, J. (1999). Emerging trends in instructional interventions. In H. D. Stolovitch & E. J. Keeps (Eds.),

Handbook of human performance technology: Improving individual and organizational performance worldwide (2nd ed., pp. 867–894). San Francisco, CA: Jossey Bass/Pfeiffer/ISPI.

Chapter 8

Some of the best books on organizational sensitivity (business etiquette) come from the Emily Post Institute. Additional information can be found at http://www.emilypost.com.

The Emily Post Institute, Inc. (2012). Emily Post [Website]. Retrieved from http://www.emilypost.com

To learn more about identifying and analyzing social interactions, check what books universities with courses in communication and organizational psychology are currently using.

Information mapping divides information to make understanding, use, and recall easier. For more information on the method and software, go to http://www.infomap.com.

Information Mapping International. (2011). Information mapping [Website]. Retrieved from http://www.infomap.com

Chapter 9

ASSIST, a web-based platform for process management, helps develop the types of measures and metrics needed to develop an accreditation plan and a performance dashboard. For more information, go to http://www.advanc-ed.org/platform-assist.

AdvanceED. (2012). ASSIST [Website]. Retrieved from http://www.advanc-ed.org/platform-assist

The IBM Reinventing Education Change Toolkit, based on the work of Dr. Elizabeth Moss-Kanter of the Harvard School of Business, can be found at http://www.reinventingeducation.org.

IBM, & Goodmeasure, Inc. (2002). Change toolkit [Website]. Retrieved from http://www.reinventingeducation.org

Chapter 10

The following publications include some of the best writings on how to sustain initiatives long enough so they institutionalize the desired behaviors:

Broad, M. L. (2005). *Beyond transfer of training: Engaging systems to improve performance*. San Francisco, CA: Pfeiffer.

Gelinas, M. V., & James, R. G. (1998). *Collaborative change: Improving organizational performance.* San Francisco, CA: Jossey-Bass/Pfeiffer.

Hale, J. A. (2003). *Performance-based management: What every manager should do to get results.* San Francisco, CA: Pfeiffer.

Hawken, P. (2010). *The ecology of commerce revised edition: A declaration of sustainability.* New York, NY: HarperCollins.

Mourier, P., & Smith, M. R. (2001). *Conquering organizational change: How to succeed where most companies fail.* Atlanta, GA: CEP Press.

Schwartz, P. (1996). *The art of the long view: Planning for the future in an uncertain world.* New York, NY: Doubleday.

References

Brinkerhoff, R. (2002). *The success case method: Find out quickly what's working and what's not.* San Francisco, CA: Berrett Kohler.

Buckingham, M., & Coffman, C. (1999). *First, break all the rules: What the world's greatest managers do differently.* New York, NY: Simon & Schuster.

Collins, J. (2001). *Good to great: Why some companies make the leap . . . and others don't.* New York, NY: Harper Business.

Corporate Leadership Council. (2004). *Driving performance and retention through employee engagement.* Arlington, VA: Corporate Executive Board.

Dewey, J. (1938). *Experience and education.* New York, NY: Macmillan.

Flanders, N. A. (1970). *Analyzing teaching behavior.* Reading, MA: Addison-Wesley.

Fournies, F. F. (2000). *Coaching for improved work performance: How to get better results from your employees, revised edition.* New York, NY: McGraw-Hill.

Gallup. (2010). *What's your engagement ratio?* Washington, DC: Gallup, Inc.

Ge, X., & Land, S. M. (2004). A conceptual framework for scaffolding ill-structured problem-solving processes using question prompts and peer interactions. *Educational Technology Research and Development, 52*(2), 5–22.

Gilmore, E. (2008). An evaluation of the efficacy of Wile's taxonomy of human performance factors (Doctoral dissertation). Available from ProQuest Dissertations and Theses database. (304606414)

Guerra-Lopez, I. J. (2008). *Performance evaluation: Proven approaches for improving program and organizational performance.* San Francisco, CA: Jossey-Bass.

Haines, A. M. (1993, Spring). Absorbent mind update: Research sheds new light on Montessori Theory. *NAMTA Journal, 18*(2), 1–25.

International Society for Performance Improvement. (2012). *10 standards of school improvement.* Retrieved on June 17, 2012, from http://www.ispi.org/content.aspx?id=1388

Kaufman, R. A., Guerra, I., & Platt, W. A. (2006). *Practical evaluation for educators: Finding what works and what doesn't.* Thousand Oaks, CA: Corwin.

Kolb, D. (1984). *Experiential learning: Experience as the source of learning and development.* Upper Saddle River, NJ: Prentice Hall.

Moon, J. (1999). *Reflection in learning and professional development: Theory and practice.* London, England: Kogan Page.

Norton, D., & Kaplan, R. (1997). *The balanced scorecard: Translating strategy into action.* Boston, MA: Harvard Business School Press.

Pink, D. H. (2009). *Drive: The surprising truth about what motivates us.* New York, NY: Riverhead Books.

Sizer, T. (1992). *Horace's school: Redesigning the American high school.* Boston, MA: Houghton Mifflin.

Wile, D. (1996). Why doers do. *Performance & Instruction, 35*(2), 30–35.

Index

Pages followed by *t* or *f* indicate tools or figures.

CORWIN
A SAGE Company

The Corwin logo—a raven striding across an open book—represents the union of courage and learning. Corwin is committed to improving education for all learners by publishing books and other professional development resources for those serving the field of PreK–12 education. By providing practical, hands-on materials, Corwin continues to carry out the promise of its motto: **"Helping Educators Do Their Work Better."**